# Contents

**Charts**

# INTRODUCTION

The Sunday School is well into its third century of ministry. From its beginning, Sunday School has endured in the face of opposition to changing times. In honor of its rich heritage, as well as the contribution of ETA's founding father Clarence Benson, you will find much of the Sunday School's historical record revived for this edition. Today's challenge to educate students in God's Word for the new millennium is surprisingly similar to the underlying concerns surrounding the earliest days of the Sunday School. By reviewing Benson's research of 1932, we gain fresh insight to a ministry that is still vital among evangelicals. Its earliest mission inspires our contemporary context.

The thesis of Benson's first edition, *The Sunday School In Action*, has remained intact through several augmentations of the course by ETA. This edition comes full circle to remind us all of common bonds with our ancestors and to challenge lay leaders for future growth. The founding principles of the Sunday School are attributed to keeping it the fortress it is today for Kingdom building.

In spite of numerous secular activities that continue to encroach on our calendars, this text unapologetically maintains the position that Sunday morning is the preferred time to conduct this ministry and the most likely time to retain the discipline of a *school*. Sunday School was so named to teach God's Word systematically and with discipline equal to, or exceeding, the formal instruction for the era. No other program attempts so broad an education in the Scriptures to *all* age levels. Amazingly the Sunday School has excelled in its execution of 2 Timothy 2:2 while staffing the movement predominantly with lay leaders.

This text specifically targets the organizational essentials that compose an effective Sunday School ministry. Lay leaders are encouraged to reference the ETA courses *Understanding Teaching* and *Teaching Techniques* for their respective philosophies and thorough commentary to administrate a Sunday School program. A full appreciation for the role of the teacher and the appropriate application of teaching methods have become full disciplines of their own and should be studied as companions to this course. This book relates the role of a Sunday School ministry to the broader task of church education.

Yvonne Thigpen,
Editor

# THE CHALLENGE

## 1

It is imperative for Christians to be centered on God's Word. A local church Sunday School program is still the most popular format to achieve this goal. Its function and purpose is directed from Deuteronomy 31:12,13 where God describes His plan, "Assemble the people—men, women and children, and the aliens living in your towns—so they can listen and learn to fear the Lord your God and follow carefully all the words of this law. Their children, who do not know this law, must hear it and learn to fear the Lord your God."

The New Testament commands to teach and study God's Word are no less direct. Jesus' words serve as the example: "Therefore go and make disciples of all nations, . . . teaching them to obey everything I have commanded you" (Matt. 28:19,20).

Today, against a background of terrorism, crime, and an uncertain future, the Sunday School must continue to disseminate the basic truths found in Scripture and bring people to a true understanding of the Gospel.

Some churches flirt with renaming the Sunday School program to something more contemporary. Some churches choose to conduct this educational effort at a time other than Sunday morning. Yet, the discipline of a Sunday morning forum remains the most popular option. Some churches develop their own curriculum materials in contrast to materials produced by denominational or independent publishing houses. Nevertheless, the essential thrust to teach and reach carries on. The Church is strengthened through strategic training programs and its most effective audience is the Sunday School program. History records this inseparable link between growth and education.

## *Development of the Sunday School*

Studying the past always helps to clarify the present and such is true regarding the Sunday School. Tribute must be paid to the efforts and sacrifices of our ancestors who paved the way for the Sunday School to be a major opportunity for Christian teaching. Sunday School remains the key educational venue for grounding evangelicals in foundational beliefs.

### Beginnings in England

Robert Raikes was a benevolent publisher in Gloucester, circa 1782, with great compassion for the poor, uneducated children who created bedlam in the streets. Raikes could have used his newspaper to condemn the laxity of parents or to demand additional protection from police authorities. Instead, he countered the circumstances by organizing an educational program to meet on a day when children and laity would not be otherwise employed.

Though his early efforts were basically trial and error, Raikes' plan called for a school to teach rudimentary academics as well as Bible knowledge. Literacy was a major concern. The poorly educated children needed hope in a variety of ways to address their desperate lives. The first location was in the kitchen of Mrs. Meredith's home in Sooty Alley, the worst slum of that area. The mere concept of educating society's misfits was considered a wild and fruitless enterprise. Few gave Raikes encouragement and many churches regarded the activity as a sacrilege for "the Sabbath Day." His friends dubbed him and his Sunday School "Bobby Wildgoose and his ragged regiment." He persisted, nevertheless, with the goal of keeping children off the streets, teaching them to read and write, and bringing them into contact with the Gospel. The only requirements to attend were that the children have clean hands and faces and combed hair. Religious instruction was enhanced as they were taken to church in the afternoon, much to the dismay of the other congregation members.

Faithful attenders were rewarded with pennies. Out of his own pocket, Raikes hired four teachers who provided instruction in reading, writing, good morals, and religion from 10:00 a.m. to 12:00 p.m. in the morning and again from 2:00 p.m. to 5:00 p.m. in the afternoon. There were many difficulties and discouragements. It was necessary for Raikes to personally quell many a riot, but he had a wonderful way with children. His distinguished appearance, no less than the cane he carried, enabled him to secure obedience and command attention.

Opposition to this new concept was gradually diminished by the publicity that Raikes was able to give the work through his periodical. His articles on the Sunday School were later reprinted in several forms as growth spread throughout Great Britain.

# SUNDAY SCHOOL

## MINISTRY

### The Church At Study

Evangelical Training Association

110 Bridge Street • Box 327

Wheaton, IL 60189-0327

Formerly titled *The Church at Study*.

Cover Design: Kurtz Design Studio, Tulsa, OK

7 6 5 4 3 2 1
6 5 4 3 2 1 0

ISBN: 0-910566-51-8

**Crossing the Atlantic**

John Wesley had already acquired a wide reputation as an evangelist in America. He also recognized the potency of Raikes' new idea for a Sunday School and immediately incorporated it into the policy of his own great undertaking. Wesley wrote, "I verily think these Sunday Schools are the noblest institutions which have been seen in Europe for some centuries, and will increase more and more, provided the teachers and instructors do their duties." Wesley went on to introduce the concept of volunteer workers. Freeing the expense of paid teachers, in turn, launched rapid growth for Sunday Schools.

The beginning of the Sunday School in North America was similar to that in England thanks to William Elliot who opened his kitchen on Sundays for teaching the children of Oak Ridge, Virginia. Various individuals encouraged his efforts until finally the church began to see the possibilities of the program.

This period of experimentation led to establishing organized conferences, called Sunday School *unions*, in the cities of Boston, New York, and Philadelphia. The objectives of these unions were to encourage teaching at the level of the child, to emphasize the value of children and youth, to promote teaching aids, and to improve classroom instruction.

**Sunday School growth in America**

As an agency, the Sunday School achieved its greatest growth and development in America. Elliott's school opened in 1785. Of course, the newly independent colonies had yet to wrestle with the issues of slavery so white children were taught at a different hour than the children of slaves. By 1801, the school was able to transfer its operation to Burton-Oak Grove Methodist Church in Brandfords Neck, Virginia, where Mr. Elliott served as its first superintendent.

A second Sunday School was established by Francis Asbury, in 1786 at the home of Thomas Crenshaw in Hanover County, Virginia. This school expressly provided for the instruction of slaves. The Methodist Conference in Charleston, South Carolina, gave official recognition to such schools in 1790, recommending sessions to operate from 6:00 a.m. to 10:00 a.m. and from 2:00 p.m. to 6:00 p.m. each Sabbath Day.

Toward the close of the eighteenth century some citizens of Philadelphia became impressed with the needs of young boys in their own city. In January of 1791, Bishop William White of the Protestant Episcopal Church was elected as the first president of a Sunday School society. By 1800, nearly two thousand pupils had been enrolled. This society became the sole source of education for many of Philadelphia's future worthy citizens.

Enthusiasm spread rapidly. As early as 1820, local Sunday

School conventions were held in the eastern states, but it was not until 1832 that the first national Sunday School convention assembled in Philadelphia. From these foundational years topics of interest included "Infant Sunday School Organization," "Qualifying Scholars to Become Teachers," and "Propriety of Having More Than One Session a Day." A second national meeting took place in Philadelphia, but a quarter century passed before the third national convention was organized. By this time, seventeen states were represented and one visitor came from Great Britain. The Civil War interfered with the fourth convention, nevertheless, in 1869 its 28 states and 526 delegates also welcomed visitors from Canada, England, Ireland, Scotland, and South Africa.

**Curriculum development**

Sunday Schools in the early years had no standard curriculum. Most of them followed the European catechetical methods stressing memory work and rote learning. The emphasis was always on the Bible but teachers were given a wide choice of content, memory passages, and classroom techniques. In 1824 the New York Sunday School Union began to produce "selected lessons" and the American Sunday School Union published the "Union Questions." This offered some uniformity but was not widespread enough to allay the forthcoming confusion of materials.

John H. Vincent and B. F. Jacobs encouraged the move toward uniformity at the ASSU convention, which ultimately led to formulating the International Lesson Committee in 1872. This committee functioned to design the International Uniform Lesson Series; consisting of the title, designated Scriptures, and the "golden text" to be studied over a seven-year period.

Finally, in 1872, the fifth national convention was held in Indianapolis to officially adopt the International Uniform Lesson, the first common curriculum to be used by multiple denominations. This endorsement was the greatest single step ever taken by the Sunday School movement and did more to standardize its work than anything previously attempted. Departmentalized lessons by independent and denominational publishers soon followed. Standardized curriculum was thereafter widely accepted

**The organized Sunday School**

The American Sunday School Union (now American Missionary Fellowship) formed in 1817 to promote lesson materials, furnish selected outlines and teaching aids. The agency also sent forth missionaries to establish rural or branch Sunday Schools throughout pioneer America. By the time the first national convention met in 1832, the ASSU had already established 2,867 schools. The Sunday School's popularity spread so rapidly it soon became an international movement as the World Sunday School Convention convened in London in 1889. The plan was for such gatherings to alternate annually between state, national, and international gatherings. In the span of one century the meager beginnings in Sooty Alley had spread throughout the world.

By contrast, the early decades of the twentieth century record the American Sunday School movement in steady decline. In 1922, the Sunday School Council of Evangelical Denominations completely merged with the International Sunday School Association to form the International Council of Religious Education. For two decades the leadership of the new organization failed to continue the promotion begun by conventions for the teaching ministry. The result was diminished inspiration and enthusiasm creating a loss of six million attenders.

Alarmed evangelicals, under the initial interest of members of the National Association of Evangelicals, organized the National Sunday School Association in 1945. Consequently, through its conventions and assistance, many regional and local associations for Sunday School improvement were formed.

## Functions of the Sunday School

The Sunday School is of immeasurable value to the church. For many decades it was fashionable to describe the Sunday School as the "teaching arm" or the "evangelism arm" of the church. Today many educators decry viewing any church program as an appendage or a part of the whole ministry. Sunday School programs emphasize the teaching role of ministry just as a missionary conference emphasizes the task of world evangelization. Yet, both are part of the Great Commission. A fragmented concept of the church is contrary to the biblical picture in Ephesians 4:1-6. The Sunday School, however, does fulfill several distinctive functions in its emphasis as the church at study.

### Reaching people

One of the primary objectives of the local church should be reaching people in the community. Visitors who attend church services, citizens who have no church affiliation and/or little training in the Word of God, and the families of the congregation all represent a rich harvest for outreach and missionary endeavor. A well-planned and carefully-executed evangelism/outreach program governs the success of growth.

Compassion to reach people for Christ must be nurtured through continued training of the entire educational staff. Inspiration is caught from its leadership. If the pastor, director, minister of education, board of Christian education, and Sunday School leadership are genuinely committed to an outreach ministry, then evangelism will be effective through the Sunday School.

The contemporary Sunday School accomplishes this task of

reaching people for Christ in a variety of ways. In most communities, and for various reasons, house-to-house canvassing is no longer an effective way to reach people. Churches have instead opted to use mail service canvassing or telephone visitation. In this way, outreach is accomplished through the promotion of the activities and study opportunities offered by the Sunday School program. One-on-one personal invitations to Sunday School are sometimes all that are needed to cultivate interest among friends and neighbors.

Some churches have developed programs that meet the interests and needs of specific segments or groups—singles, divorced, widowed, single parents, handicapped, elderly—as a common point of interest to involve them in the church, teach God's Word, and ultimately witness their salvation. As with Robert Raikes, reaching out involves leadership who respond to a need, set an example, delegate responsibilities, and train workers to do an effective job.

### Teaching people

The Sunday School's main thrust today is to teach the Bible so that people may be brought into a personal relationship with the Lord Jesus Christ. Teaching the Word of God is the supreme motive and desire of those involved in Christian education. The entire Sunday School staff must recognize and commit to this task. Teachers have the opportunity and obligation to bring their students into a personal relationship with Christ as Savior and Lord. Since the Bible is the Sunday School's textbook, and it alone presents the Christian way of life and access into the presence of God, the Sunday School is supremely important for developing study skills and comprehension.

### Equipping people

If a Sunday School ministry is really on target, it results in a church that regards equipping individuals to serve Christ through the local church as one of its ultimate obligations. Growth in Christ must include stewardship and dedication to service. A total equipping ministry includes teaching the Word of God, developing and practicing godly living, and emphasizing the principles of service. Later chapters in this book will explore these topics more fully.

## *Purposes of the Sunday School*

In the last half of the twentieth century, defining the purposes of church education shifted considerably. Many churches failed to recognize the place of the Sunday School in meeting their educational objectives. The church's leadership, including the pastoral staff, are charged with teaching the Word of God and must continually evaluate the direction in which the church's total educational program is moving. Programs help local congregations achieve specific needs, yet many churches have over-programmed their members. It is imperative for the challenge of Deuteronomy 31 to find a voice in our contemporary education. The following brief list of major church educational objectives is representative of the Sunday School's great task.

## Attain a personal knowledge of the Trinity

Church education helps the individual see God the Father as sovereign, infinite, eternal, and unchanging in His being; recognize all His attributes including holiness, justice, goodness, truth, and love; and accept Him as the creator and rightful owner of the universe. This aim should be properly interpreted to the various age levels so that students can understand God as the heavenly Father who is personally interested in His children's welfare and who has a master plan for each person.

Jesus Christ is God. When this is recognized, Christ can rightly be seen and served as Lord and Master. Christ is the head of the Church and a friend and advocate who pleads the sinner's case before God the Father. His coming, death, and resurrection perfected our salvation. A personal experience with Him is vital to eternal life and forgiveness of sin.

Sunday School students must be taught that the Holy Spirit is the third person of the Trinity, possessing the attributes of God. Students should learn the Holy Spirit convicts of sin, provides assurance of salvation, and baptizes them into the Body of Christ. The Christian educator will teach the Holy Spirit's role as indweller, controller, and the one who empowers every believer in Christ, revealing the deeper things of God's Word.

## Develop a vibrant Christian life

Living daily for Christ, in the power of the Holy Spirit and according to God's Word, necessitates a growing spiritual life characterized by daily devotion. Social life must conform to the standards of Christian conduct presented in the Word of God. This also involves biblical instruction that results in seeking the Lord's will for all important life decisions.

## Understand God's Word

People need to be taught that the Bible is the complete, authoritative, infallible revelation from God to mankind which convicts us of sin, reveals the plan of salvation that produces faith in Christ, and nourishes Christian growth. People need to experience the Word of God supplying truth for daily living. The Bible also offers comfort in all of life's experiences and ultimately increases our love for Christ, thus guiding us into His image.

## Appreciate our heritage

Church education should include the use of Christian literature, music, and art. A confused world needs the stabilizing effect of Christians and their philosophy on cultural patterns. A unified and articulate Christian philosophy, with a biblical interpretation of life, is society's only remedy for death and destruction.

### Achieve loyalty to the church

Loyalty necessitates adequate instruction about the Church as the Body of Christ and each believer's responsibility to Christ as the head of the Church. An effective Sunday School emphasizes the local congregation as the hub of the Christian community and encourages participation in all its ministries.

### Communicate responsibility for communities

Church education helps believers to make Christ known through individual witness and cooperative expression on moral convictions. Christian influence should be felt in every area of human endeavor and life as a whole—the Christian home, schools and colleges, hospitals, civic activities, employer/employee relationships.

### Become global Christians

The impact of the Bible's mission is inescapable. Therefore, church education nurtures people in dedication of their lives; yielding time, talents, wealth, and will to God. As God's truth is taught, people will be led into the service of sharing God's Word throughout the world under the Holy Spirit's direction. The Sunday School fulfills the purpose of Christian education to enlarge the church's total ministry.

## *Summary*

From its humble beginnings in England and America, the Sunday School has fulfilled a vital need. Today, it is the most effective educational ministry in churches throughout many parts of the world. The role of the Sunday School is carried out through reaching, teaching, and equipping.

Though many forces have sought to uproot the Sunday School, it has endured and remains strong. The Sunday School maintains its historical purpose of bringing men, women, and children to a personal knowledge of the triune God. Sunday School has persisted in stressing the value of a vibrant Christian life based on the precepts of God's Word. The Sunday School has also encouraged the appreciation of our rich Christian heritage as well as the present responsibility to our church, community, and the entire world.

With principles and purposes like these, is it any wonder that the Lord has blessed the Sunday School for over 200 years?

## *For Further Discussion*

1. Why is Sunday School imperative?
2. What is the role of the Sunday School?
3. Briefly sketch how the Sunday School developed.
4. What are the main purposes of the Sunday School?
5. How does the Word of God impact the Sunday School?
6. What are the major church educational objectives?

## *For Application*

1. Involve the group in a Bible search for verses or sections of Scripture that fortify the major Sunday School objectives at your church.
2. Survey people who have recently started attending your Sunday School to determine how they first heard of your Sunday School or church. Based on these findings determine a plan for expanding your Sunday School's outreach activities to address student needs.
3. Examine the class rolls of the children's Sunday School classes at your church to determine if you are reaching potential adult Sunday School students at your church.
4. Examine the aims of several individual lessons in your Sunday School curriculum to determine if the major purposes of the Sunday School are addressed.
5. Reword the educational objectives for your church to consider each age level. Give particular interest to evaluating the age level where you presently minister.

# Sunday School Time Line

|  |  |
|------|-------|
| 1780 | Beginning in England |
| 1790 | Beginning in America |
| 1800 | |
| 1810 | |
| 1817 | American Sunday School Union |
| 1820 | |
| 1824 | New York Sunday School Union |
| 1830 | |
| 1832 | First National Sunday School Convention |
| 1840 | |
| 1850 | |
| 1860 | |
| 1870 | |
| 1872 | International Uniform Lessons |
| 1880 | |
| 1889 | World Sunday School Convention |
| 1890 | |
| 1900 | |
| 1910 | |
| 1920 | |
| 1922 | International Council of Religious Education |
| 1930 | ETTA, now ETA founded |
| 1940 | |
| 1945 | National Sunday School Association |
| 1950 | |
| 1960 | |
| 1970 | |
| 1980 | 200th Anniversary of the Sunday School |
| 1990 | |
| 2000 | |

# MINISTRY GOAL: EVANGELIZING

## 2

The next three chapters are concerned with Sunday School ministry goals, all of which come from Christ's Great Commission: "Therefore go and make disciples of all nations, baptizing them in the name of the Father and of the Son and of the Holy Spirit, and teaching them to obey everything I have commanded you. And surely I am with you always, to the very end of the age" (Matt. 28:19,20). As Christ indicates here, the overall goal of Sunday School ministry is to facilitate making disciples. In order to achieve this goal there are three subordinate and progressive goals—evangelizing, edifying, and equipping. This chapter considers the first one—evangelizing.

The Sunday School is responsible to reach out into its surrounding community—"Therefore go and make disciples of all nations." The average Sunday School is lacking here. When a Sunday School conducts an effective evangelism program, it reaches the entire church family and surrounding community. In addition, it starts a multiplication process that results in demonstrating tremendous possibilities for Christ's Great Commission.

### *Prerequisites for evangelism*
Every leader and teacher is responsible for reaching the Sunday School's constituency. This important task can transform the church, the community, the country, and the world. Several prerequisites are necessary for this process to catch fire in the context of a Sunday School.

### Enlarged faith

The great conquests of the church are accomplished by faith. Those who believe God have "conquered kingdoms, administered justice, and gained what was promised; who shut the mouths of lions" (Heb. 11:33) and built great Sunday Schools. "With God all things are possible" (Matt. 19:26).

### Vision of the unreached

Matthew 9:35 reveals that Jesus went about doing good, reaching and teaching people. Matthew 9:36 notes that Jesus Himself had compassion as He viewed people, stating that they were harassed and helpless like sheep without a shepherd. What was the problem? Evidently, at that time, there were not enough willing workers who had a vision for their lost condition. According to Jesus, "The harvest is plentiful but the workers are few" (Matt. 9:37). A vision for the lost condition of unreached people in the community is absolutely necessary for the church to begin attaining the goal of evangelism.

### Compassion for the lost

When Scripture reports that Jesus had compassion on the people, it also indicates that this was not merely a sudden or passing emotion. This attitude was constant with the Lord. In order for churches to reach their community, its leadership must recognize the need of people to accept Christ as Savior.

The Christian's compassion should match Christ's commission. A positive, strong desire to lead people to Christ and have them accept Him as Savior must begin in the lives of those leading and teaching in the Sunday School. When leaders and teachers exhibit compassion and an awareness of people's need to accept Christ, this contagion spreads to the entire church membership. Truly, love is a constraining force. But this love involves not only a love *for* God, but a love *of* God for those who are outside His fold. When a church or a Sunday School stops seeking, it ceases growing.

### Understanding the value of a person

Sunday School leaders and teachers should be well aware of the value which the Lord places upon the individual. The Word of God says that we are worth more than sparrows (Luke 12:7) and above the value of sheep (Matt. 12:12). Christ also used strong statements in an effort to help people understand an individual's value. "What good will it be for a man if he gains the whole world, yet forfeits his soul? Or what can a man give in exchange for his soul?" (Matt. 16:26). Considering the *faith*, the *field*, the *need*, and the *value* of each individual, reaching people is not merely a question of convenience, but on the basis of the Word of God, a divine mandate.

### Preparation for new students

The average Sunday School puts forth only meager, spasmodic efforts to increase its enrollment. In past decades some schools conducted an occasional contest. Competition ran high for a time as students worked to win a prize. Such methods may have accomplished an immediate purpose, but they were not completely effective in building permanent enrollment and attendance.

Consecrated, carefully-equipped and trained leaders and teachers maintain Sunday School enrollment and build attendance. When leaders and teachers commit themselves to evangelism, pray for its effectiveness, and are involved in implementing it, Sunday Schools grow. Instruction in the principles of evangelism is as important for Sunday School workers as instruction in teaching methodology and age level characteristics.

Planning is essential if a church is to adequately handle increased attendance. What will the church do with an increase in attendance? A new or remodeled educational unit may be needed. The goal is making disciples, not just contacting visitors.

## Personnel involved in evangelism

Regular church attendance is a major factor in achieving the goal of effective evangelism. An early contact with the Sunday School makes it easier to help adults accept Christ and be assimilated into the Body. But tragically only a small percentage of students are converted during classtime. Lack of evangelistic fervor is partly to blame. The home and the church must share the task of evangelism equally for effectiveness. Encouragement comes in knowing that this small fraction of Sunday School converts eventually constitute three-fourths of church membership. The other one-fourth of church membership is largely composed of adult converts who at some time were under the ministry of the Sunday School.

Those who are influential in helping people come to know Christ as Savior through Sunday School ministry are: pastors, parents, and Sunday School teachers and leaders.

### Pastors

Effective evangelism begins with pastors who are committed to Sunday School evangelism. Though many Sunday Schools seek to grow, most have no systematic evangelism emphasis and effort. Pastors, in cooperation with all Sunday School staff members, should prepare practical, perennial programs, providing for vital relationships with parents, teachers, leaders, the school, and the church membership class.

As representatives of Sunday Schools, pastors introduce parents to those spiritual elements which nourish growing children and prepare them to become believers in Christ. In their visitation and consultations, pastors learn of family problems and carry their burdens in prayer. They encourage parents to live their Christian faith in their family life, witness to their own faith in Christ, and find practical ways to encourage their children to accept Him as their Savior.

Next to their ministry with parents, pastors work with Sunday School leaders and teachers. These lay volunteers hold the key to effective evangelism. Teachers who first win their students' confidence will then be more effective in guiding their spiritual matters. This is especially true with teens who are sometimes reticent or unwilling to confide in their parents.

The responsibility of pastors only begins with their own evangelism efforts. It continues as they also receive communication about those who have accepted Christ as Savior through the efforts of others. Then, as soon as possible, personal interviews can answer the new believer's questions or doubts and ascertain their comprehension of their decision for Christ. Often, as an outgrowth of these consultations, church membership or new believers' classes help pastors accomplish this important part of their ministries.

## Parents

In every generation, fathers and mothers hold the key to evangelizing their own children. When parents possess genuine spiritual leadership, are equipped and trained in the principles of effective evangelism, and are confident in their skills, the children willingly accompany them to church and many make early decisions for Christ.

## Sunday School teachers and leaders

Although not all believers have the spiritual gift of evangelism, all are called to witness for Christ. This is especially true of Sunday School teachers and leaders. In order for teachers and leaders to be effective as witnesses, they must be equipped and trained. They must understand that God has called them to witness for Christ to their students. They must be equipped to perform this task efficiently and enthusiastically. They should know the steps to be followed in witnessing to students and leading them to Christ.

Teachers often keep a notebook with a separate page for each student. On these pages teachers might record such data as the student's name, address, school grade, birthday, picture, phone number, home life, interests, hobbies, ambitions, and spiritual progress. These records can then be used as a convenient prayer reminder and will help make prayers more specific.

To be effective witnesses, teachers and leaders need first to win the students' respect. They must enter into the students' lives and seek to share with them. They then seek to become friends with their students. They show interest in the students individually and also as a group. They talk with their students as they assemble and establish friendships which also helps win their confidence. Most educators feel that the most important time teachers spend with their students is before class begins. For this reason, teachers should be in the classroom before the first student arrives.

## *Productivity of evangelism*

Three elements can be identified in developing a productive program of Sunday School outreach—prayer, godly living, and biblical methodology. If these three elements are kept in proper balance and priority, an evangelism program will be effective.

### Prayer

The most important ingredient of effective Sunday School evangelism is a praying church. Throughout the Book of Acts when the infant church was developing, the power of prayer was constantly stressed and experienced in believers' lives. Prayer is no less important for the people of God today.

When teachers and leaders pray for their students and tell their classes they are praying for them and why, Sunday School students come to Christ. If only one thing can be done about Sunday School evangelism, let it be a sincere and systematic program of prayer.

### Godly living

Good teachers and leaders will not limit their ministries to Sunday morning activities. They know that they cannot evangelize their students simply by what they say. Students need to observe consecrated Christian lives. The old adage declares, "You speak so loud by what you are that I cannot hear what you say."

When students are ill, they appreciate every attention that is shown, and because illness curtails outside interests, they are most amenable to instruction. Calling on sick and shut-in students will do more to win their love and respect than any amount of formal instruction. Moreover, visits to the home will give teachers firsthand knowledge of the students' home environments and a better understanding of how to reach them.

Teachers are more able to win their students' respect and love when they participate in their social events. An evening or a Sunday afternoon interacting with a class planning recreational programs and participating with them are often the most productive times teachers ever spend with their students. One fifth-grade teacher took his students to camp and spent two weeks with them. He played with them, laughed with them, and ate with them. He also witnessed to them of his faith in Christ. As a result, 13 of the 15 later came to profess faith in Christ and joined the church.

## Biblical methodology

The early church knew nothing of inviting designated visitors. Its people were witnesses on location wherever they came in contact with unbelievers. To be sure, now that churches have specific places and times for worship, emphasis on evangelism takes place more often among the gathered church. It is a fact of contemporary evangelicalism that our methods for productive ways to evangelize have changed.

In addition to teaching God's Word, counseling, visitation, and informal contacts with students help evangelistic Sunday School teachers and leaders to accomplish community outreach.

Publicity prepares the way for personal contact. It is comparatively easy to establish a point of contact in a community that is well informed about the life and work of a growing church and its educational program. A variety of publicity types effectively inform the community about the church and its program. Some churches and Sunday Schools find newspaper advertisements work well in attracting people from the community to their activities. Others use posters, flyers, radio announcements, or even house-to-house canvasses. Newcomer lists are readily available for people transferring into an area. Best results often are achieved by using a combination of approaches. The most effective, however, is personal contact—one person inviting another to attend church and Sunday School with them.

Whatever the source of the contact, after it has been made it is important to get basic data regarding each person who visits the church or Sunday School. This includes the visitor's name, address, and children's names and ages (if applicable). Often churches and Sunday Schools design and print index cards with these categories printed on them.

A special follow-up committee should then investigate and evaluate all information secured about the visitors. The committee should then classify the prospective students and families by departments and classes and develop a follow-up procedure.

All teachers and leaders should recognize their position in the Sunday School is a strategic one for evangelism. The desired principles and techniques should be a vital part of the equipping and training program. The church contributes to effective Sunday School evangelism by providing such training yet the pastor's personal interest will be reflected in the teachers' and leaders' attitudes. Fall planning conferences or retreats should include opportunities to encourage teachers and leaders to "do the work of an evangelist."

## Summary

Although shared by the overall church's mission, Christ's mandate to "make disciples" is also the Sunday School's task. The initial step or goal to accomplishing this task is evangelism.

In order for the Sunday School to reach this goal, several prerequisites are necessary: a faith that believes growth can be accomplished; a vision for the unreached; a deep compassion for those who do not know the Lord; an appreciation of an individual's value; and a building prepared to handle increased enrollment.

In order for Sunday School evangelism to be effective, the whole staff must be involved—pastor, leaders, teachers, and (in the case of children) parents.

Pastors are responsible to promote evangelism among their staff, in the congregation, and through personal contacts in homes. Pastors need to be involved in evangelism from the point of initial contact through to church membership classes.

Parents hold the key to their children accepting Christ as Savior. Surveys point out that the largest number of young people who accept Christ come from Christian homes.

The key to Sunday School teachers' and leaders' effectiveness as witnesses for Christ is their rapport with their classes. If they capture their students' respect and love, they have a greater chance of leading them to Christ. Training in evangelism principles and techniques will also increase effectiveness.

For an evangelism goal to be productive, three elements are necessary; a praying church that seeks the Lord in its processes; the witness of godly lives by those involved in the process; and biblical methodology in carrying it out.

## For Further Discussion

1. How is regular church attendance related to effective evangelism?
2. Why should Sunday School evangelism be of interest to pastors?
3. How can pastors enlist the parents' support in evangelism?
4. Why should every teacher be trained in evangelism principles and techniques?
5. How are teachers and leaders keys to Sunday School evangelism?
6. How does church and Sunday School program publicity affect its evangelism efforts?
7. Why is reporting of evangelism program contacts essential?
8. Who is responsible for the information secured from evangelism contacts?

## *For Application*

1. How would you lead a child to Christ? A young person? An adult?
2. Evaluate the program of evangelism in your Sunday School. What are its strengths and weaknesses? What can be done to improve its effectiveness?
3. Carefully survey your last quarter's curriculum materials noting at what points evangelistic opportunities were presented in your lesson plans. Then evaluate your reaction to these as you review what you did in class at that particular point. Also, examine the material for the forthcoming quarter, carefully noting those lessons which readily lend themselves to evangelism within the classroom.

# MINISTRY GOAL: EDIFYING

## 3

In the previous chapter, evangelism was considered as the first step or goal of a Sunday School ministry. The second is edifying or building up faith in Christ. Sunday School ministry begins by confronting people with the truth of the Gospel. Accepting this truth, however, is just the beginning. The Sunday School must be prepared to teach God's Word to believers. The Lord's commission to make disciples involves this area of edification—teaching the Word of God.

### *Prerequisites for edification*

Leaders and teachers must possess several qualities if they are to carry on the process of spiritual growth.

#### Lives that reflect Christ

To build up other believers, we must first influence them with our own lives. No one except Christ is perfect. Teachers and leaders must be rooted in the faith themselves before they can lead others into spiritual growth.

Paul told Titus to be an example of good works (Titus 2:7). The word *tupon* is translated "example" and literally means "a pattern;" something a person would lay down and trace around to create a duplicate. Those who help others grow in the faith need to have lives that are worthy of being copied. People are more encouraged to live the Christian life when they see it modeled in others.

**Time to spend with students**

Looking at Christ's example reveals a two-to-three year time period of total dedication to twelve men. Sunday School teachers usually cannot spend two to three years daily with their students. However helping them build up their faith does require more than a one-hour-per-week commitment. The edification process demands getting to know students both in class and other settings. Building up students is sometimes easier to accomplish while meeting informally during the week than in the structured classroom atmosphere.

Christ was a leader, teacher, adviser, and guide to those He discipled. He was also their friend as expressed in John 15:14. Sunday School teachers who have not become their students' friends have done little to build them up in the faith. Teachers who become friends to their students not only share content from God's Word but also find many opportunities to help them experience continual spiritual growth.

## *Personnel involved in edification*

The Sunday School's ministry comprises much of the educational program. Evangelism is the initial objective; but edification should be the bulk of the ministry. Sunday School personnel should be committed to their students' spiritual development.

**Pastors**

Pastors, by virtue of their leadership roles, encourage spiritual growth each week from the pulpit. Complementary goals are shared between the church at large and its educational ministries. Pastors must advise parents on building up their children in the faith. They should counsel and pray with parents, as that is who will have the strongest impact for guiding their children's spiritual growth. If the pastor's own life is a shining example of what it means to follow Christ, he will truly be a "people edifier."

Pastoral responsibilities begin with studies centered on developing the Christian life and stewardship. In most churches, these classes nurture the initial spiritual growth process and serve as an introduction to church membership.

**Parents**

As in the case of evangelism, Christian parents have the primary role to feed and nurture their children in the things of God. Their faith is constantly on display before their children. As pointed out previously, the majority of children coming from Christian homes are significantly influenced to accept the Lord through their parents' example. It is also true that parents, through opportunities for Bible study and prayer in the home, continue the discipling efforts of the church. Sadly many Christian homes shun devotional times as part of the family's regular activities together. If children are not spiritually fed by their parents, it becomes necessary for the Sunday School to provide leadership for edification.

### Teachers and leaders

If the teachers and leaders are prepared with the principles and techniques of evangelism, they will be instrumental in their students' spiritual growth.

The key to fulfilling the teacher's role in edifying students rests in developing personal relationships. If teachers show sincere concern for growth in the Lord, their students will respond. Time spent getting to know students outside of class produces a desire to know more about the Christian life.

Above all, teachers should be genuine. More is accomplished by taking an honest approach to the difficulties in life. All teachers are occasionally tempted and frustrated and their lives are not completely free from problems. Students appreciate openness and honesty. Those who teach children can share how they felt while growing up. Students will feel closer to teachers they perceive as human, yet able to overcome problems through the power of Christ.

## *Principles for productivity*

Three elements are imperative for developing productive edification goals in the Sunday School: prayer, knowledge of the Bible, and patience. If these three elements are found in the lives of teachers, leaders, and parents, they will make a large contribution toward the program's effectiveness.

### Prayer

It has been said, "When all else fails—pray." How much better for the principle to be, "Before everything else fails—pray." The importance of prayer in Sunday School ministry cannot be stressed enough. The church's future depends on a constant supply of mature Christians to carry on its ministries. The ministry of building up people in the faith needs prayer support in all Sunday School departmental and general meetings as well as in weekly congregational prayer meetings. As individuals throughout the church regularly pray, many will be strengthened.

Again and again Scripture points us to the value of prayer. Throughout His ministry, Jesus prayed for those He led. Paul mentions many times that he was praying for the members of the churches he helped found. Teachers and leaders who are involved in edifying others should be people of prayer who constantly bring their students' needs before the Lord.

## Knowledge of the Bible

While proficiency as a Bible scholar is not a requirement for a teaching ministry, diligent attention to Bible study is essential. Teachers and leaders who seek to help students grow spiritually must themselves be students of the Word. To help a new believer in faith development, the Sunday School teacher needs to know the Bible—the sourcebook of the Christian life. A three-fold understanding of God's Word is necessary for every teacher and leader.

The first is *doctrine*. Teachers and leaders need a working knowledge of foundational biblical doctrines such as the incarnation and deity of Christ, the authority and inspiration of the Bible, and the way to salvation for all mankind. A firm foundation in the Word of God will help others deepen their convictions in spiritual matters.

The second is *Bible background*. Teachers and leaders not only need to understand the Word but must also have a grasp of the Bible's background and history. This knowledge will strengthen their understanding of the biblical message.

The third is *how the Bible relates to life*. A grasp of how the Bible applies to the problems and relationships of life is crucial. Teachers and leaders must be able to point students to the place in the Bible where they can find the answers to the difficulties they face.

All three of these areas of Bible knowledge require disciplined study and readiness from teachers and leaders. Students' lives will evidence the benefits of preparation in these areas.

## Patience

When it comes to growth in grace—edification—patience is not just a virtue, it is a necessity. Students assimilate information, apply knowledge, and make it part of their everyday behavior at different rates and by different learning styles. Because one student makes great strides toward growing up in the Lord and another seemingly takes small steps does not mean that one teacher or leader is effective and another is not. The Lord works His plan differently with each individual. Perhaps tomorrow, next week, next month, or even years later, growth will be evident. The Lord will produce results in His time.

# *Summary*

The second step or goal in discipling persons for Christ is edifying—building them up in the faith.

Since this process is so vital to fulfilling Sunday School ministry goals, everyone needs to be involved. Valuable prerequisites for those leading the program are: lives that reflect Christ, time to spend with students, and a willingness to be a friend.

Three groups of people are instrumental in an effective ministry of edification—pastors, parents, and teachers. Pastors should be constantly helping their congregations to grow in the faith from their pulpits, personal interaction, and in guiding the Sunday School staff. As with other ministries among children, parents need to be involved in lending support to the program and in carrying out its process in the home. Effective teachers for edification exhibit lives that illustrate their words, gain their students' love and respect, spend time with their students outside of class, and are honest in relating their own shortcomings and failures.

Principles for productivity in an edification program are: prayer for and about the program, a strong knowledge of the Bible, and patience on the part of all concerned.

## *For Further Discussion*

1.  What is the primary responsibility of the Sunday School ministry?
2.  Why must everyone in the Sunday School be committed to the program of edification?
3.  Why must the edifier's life be rooted and grounded in the faith?
4.  How can teachers and leaders find ways to spend time with the students outside of class?
5.  Why is it important for teachers and leaders to be the students' friends?
6.  How can parents help their children to grow spiritually?
7.  How can a teacher avoid appearing phony?
8.  What three levels of Bible knowledge should teachers and leaders have attained?
9.  Why is patience so important for an edification program to be effective?

## *For Application*

1.  Evaluate how well your Sunday School students are evidencing spiritual growth.
2.  Design a specific one-year edification program for your class. If you have a small class, you might be able to work on a personal basis with each student over the next year. If your class is large, you may want to design discipling partnerships whereby more mature class members work with less-advanced students under your supervision.

# MINISTRY GOAL: EQUIPPING

## 4

The Sunday School's primary ministry is discipling students. The previous two chapters considered the first two goals in the process—evangelism and edification. This chapter deals with the third and ultimate goal—equipping students to serve Christ. Bringing people to faith in Christ and building them up in this faith is not enough. Before Sunday School ministry can feel it has accomplished its goals, it must equip students to go out themselves and make disciples. When this final goal is reached the church reproduces itself. "And the things you have heard me say in the presence of many witnesses entrust to reliable men who will also be qualified to teach others" (2 Tim. 2:2). Failure to perpetuate the process produces seriously ineffective Christians and massive shortages of qualified workers throughout the church's ministries.

## *Prerequisites for equipping*

To carry out effective equipping ministries, Sunday Schools must produce students who are maturing spiritually, teachers who are faithful, and programs that encourage ministry involvement.

### Students who are maturing spiritually

In Ephesians 4, Paul clearly identifies the task of church and Sunday School leadership "for the *equipping* of the saints for the work of service, to the building up of the body of Christ; until we all attain to the unity of the faith, and of the knowledge of the Son of God, to a mature man, to the measure of the stature which belongs to the fulness of Christ" (Eph. 4:12,13 NASB). Note the inseparable relationship between knowledge and behavior. We grow in knowledge, become mature, and thereby are equipped to perform works of service.

28

Knowledge has to do with information. In the case of Christian growth, information about the Bible and the truth about God and man lay the foundation not only for salvation, but for Christian growth. Simply processing this knowledge does not produce change in students. Students must believe what they have learned for it to affect their lives. Then, because students believe certain things, they formulate values and begin acting within the framework of those values. This is an important goal for maturing students—seeking to live according to biblical standards.

## Teachers who are faithful

People tend to gravitate toward glamour ministries, particularly those that produce visible and immediate results. Those who have selected Sunday School ministry know that it is a long-term, sometimes tedious, but always critical field of service. Patience is an essential quality faithful teachers must possess.

Teaching is central to biblical ministry. Jesus Himself was called the master teacher. In His post-resurrection appearance on the Emmaus Road, He expounded the Scriptures (Luke 24:27) and the central emphasis in His Great Commission is on teaching (Matt. 28:20). In Paul's list of gifts of the Spirit, teaching is permanently united with pastoral work: "It was He who gave . . . some to be pastors and teachers" (Eph. 4:11).

Students will not be ready to begin serving the Lord after reading through the Gospels once. Nor will a year or two of Sunday School totally equip them to begin serving Christ. Note how God has worked with His people through the ages. Moses spent forty years in the desert in addition to his forty years in one of the major urban centers of the world. The apostle Paul had a brilliant education in Greek culture and Hebrew theology but was set aside for preparation before he was qualified to serve the Lord. The disciples struggled and failed for over three years before any significant positive results of their ministries became evident.

God has never been in a hurry to produce effective servants. He has always been patient with our failures, frustrations, and futility. Why then are Sunday School teachers and leaders less faithful to their students, sometimes impatient for them to attain a level of spiritual maturity? Spiritual maturity is a life process, not a final destination.

Sometimes it requires trying various methods to see if they work. Some teachers find discussion works best, while others might find students respond better to role play activities or buzz groups. Finding appropriate methods is important but it does not replace the work of the Holy Spirit in teaching. To advance students from the content level to the application level requires reliance on the Spirit of God. Dedication to study involves the students' use of activities and materials which emphasize involvement and interaction, training classes, counseling with others, and huge quantities of prayer.

**Programs that encourage involvement in ministry**

Some Sunday Schools are satisfied with students who achieve content—such as knowing Bible stories and quoting verses accurately. Other Sunday Schools strive for a large attendance and emphasize the fellowship. Sunday Schools interested in carrying out the biblical mandate to equip their students to serve Christ *must* be schools that set this goal with emphasis.

Sunday School has the greatest potential for acquainting students with ways to serve Christ and in giving them opportunities for cultivating and practicing their service skills. Sunday Schools that provide these opportunities encourage students to participate in various ministries, both big and small, even while they are growing spiritually.

Sunday School students from the youngest to the oldest can serve the Lord. Spiritual seeds have been planted by preschool children who explain Jesus' love to their friends and family. Elementary school students will be more likely to spread the word about God's love among their peers in school, on the playground, and at home if Sunday School has introduced them to a variety of application activities. Students of any age seldom serve in these ways if they have never been challenged beyond the level of acquired knowledge. Sunday Schools provide instruction, encouragement, and activities that emphasize participation to fulfill their educational goals and reap the benefits in growth.

## *Personnel involved in equipping*

Active service equips others to become involved in ministry. Keeping this in mind, the whole Sunday School team—pastors, parents, and Sunday School workers—works together to produce the atmosphere of joyful service.

**Pastors**

The primary role of pastors in the equipping ministry is supporting and encouraging the congregation. Their role begins with the evangelism goals, continues with involvement in edification goals, to climax with emphasizing ways Christians can serve Christ. This can be done from the pulpit, in counseling situations, or personal interaction. Above all, pastors need to be sure they illustrate effective service for Christ. Pastors are the best models of mature Christians who have choosen a career of serving Christ. For this reason, they should make themselves available for counseling Sunday School students who have questions concerning vocational Christian ministry.

**Parents**

The role of parents in the equipping process is also primarily one of example. Much of ministering for Christ can be done as family activities. Unfortunately, many of today's Christian families, who operate under the pressure of two careers and full school schedules, often find little time for each other and even less for joint Christian ministry. This increases the Sunday School's responsibility to provide leadership and counsel to families as they set new priorities.

**Sunday School staff**

If equipping students to serve Christ is the ultimate goal of Sunday School ministry, teachers need to be the prime motivators. Some teachers simply do not understand the principle of involvement in the teaching/learning process. Often the section of the lesson plan that stresses how to respond to scriptural truth is left at the end of the lesson plan. Application activities are ignored and, as a result, a vital connection for students is lost. When teachers are busy with full-time jobs, as well as families, they do not have out-of-class time to see students demonstrate their faith. It is important to challenge students with a specific application.

Whatever the age or degree of maturity, students need to be equipped and involved in ministry. Sometimes enlisting students in group activities which help them to minister outside the classroom accomplishes the equipping goal, but this calls for more than the one-hour-per-week class time. For young children to become involved in group ministry projects, the teacher must accompany them or guide them as they work in a group. Individual students may need help in fulfilling their tasks. Time spent in equipping students to serve Christ in their world, however, is never wasted.

Most Sunday School curriculum materials provide lesson-related suggestions to help students practice and respond to lesson truths. Teachers who utilize these ideas find their students' spiritual experiences are broadened and their faith becomes more meaningful.

For some students in the Sunday School, the teacher may be the only role model they see. Students from non-Christian homes need to observe how to minister for Christ. Teachers can show special attention to these students and encourage them to demonstrate their faith. Teachers who become their students' friends will find it easier to equip them for ministry.

Enlist the aid of leadership, assistants or team teachers, the media center director, the mission coordinator, and others to provide ideas and suggestions for service opportunities. To reach the goal of equipping students to serve Christ, Sunday School leaders need to work together on activities in the teaching/learning process. Involve all students in some form of Christian ministry.

In departmental and general staff meetings, superintendents should stress with teachers and other staff members the importance of using student participation. Since many teachers may not be experienced in these methods, leaders should use these meetings as training for teachers and other staff members. As they feel more confident using different approaches to learning, they will realize the need to get students past the level of knowledge and on to personal application.

ETA's *Church Membership Program* provides a cost-effective way to maximize the effectiveness of the church's adult education program by encouraging regular training sessions. Benefits include twelve prepared workshops covering various topics. These workshops include an audio tape as well as reproducible handouts. Subsequent year members receive video seminars. The overall goal of the *Church Membership Program* is to encourage the church to be consistent in its training of its teachers.

Sunday School leaders should also strive to involve as many people as possible in the Sunday School ministry. Many jobs need to be done: teaching, assisting, playing instruments, leading worship activities, record keeping, etc. All these opportunities provide outlets for persons to minister in the church. It is the leaders' responsibility to help people get involved.

## *Principles for productivity*

Three key elements are important to attaining the goal of equipping students to serve Christ: challenging students to greater faith, being enthusiastic, and emphasizing further training.

### Challenge students to greater faith

When Christ equipped His disciples for ministry, He showed His love for them by explaining He was going to prepare a place for them. He said that He would send the Holy Spirit to help them and informed them of the privilege of prayer. He also conveyed warmth, personal interest, concern, and acceptance.

After assuring students that Christ will be with them in all they do, suggest small ways they can begin ministering to their world. Increase these ideas according to the students' maturity, responses, and success. As students become involved, they will be motivated to do more. Place students in positions where they need to trust God and expose them to situations where their faith will be tested. When they succeed victoriously in small ways, they will be challenged to do greater things for God.

For students who desire to read about other people who lived by faith, have books available that show how men and women have trusted God in times past. Introduce students to other mature Christians who can share their story of God's work in their life.

**Be enthusiastic**

Enthusiasm is a great motivator. Sunday School students need to observe people who are enthusiastically living the Christian life and involved in ministry. Teachers who relate how exciting living for Christ can be greatly influence their students to step out in faith and begin serving Christ in their world. Teachers and leaders need to share ministry triumphs and also invite other people into the classroom who will testify of the Lord's provision in their lives.

Above all, give students a purpose for ministering for Christ. Explain to your students that God wants to use them in meaningful ways.

**Emphasize further training**

Equipping students for ministry can be done within the Sunday School and church program. However for people who desire to serve in leadership capacities, further training is preferable. This training can take many forms. Many churches identify the standards for volunteer leadership positions. Training might take the form of correspondence courses, conferences, or ETA's *Church Ministry Certificate Program*.

Churches might determine an excellent program for equipping volunteers is achievable with a Bible institute in their church. Establishing an institute of this type is not synonymous with a major academic school operation. A Bible institute can be established whenever a local church is committed to a regular curriculum of quality instruction. Several churches in a community do, however, often work together to develop a community institute. The goal of these institutes is perpetuation of quality for lay leadership.

With careful planning, the institute can be a useful tool of God that offers balanced and thorough training for ministry, sound teaching, and encouragement for continued preparation.

For those whose goal is vocational Christian ministry, Bible school, college, or seminary training is essential. Teachers in the youth department should keep themselves informed of good Bible schools and colleges to recommend so their students make wise decisions.

## *Summary*

The Sunday School's ministry is not complete until students are fully equipped to minister for Christ.

To accomplish this, several prerequisites must be evident: students who are growing spiritually, teachers who exhibit faithfulness, not requiring that all students be ready to minister at the same time and in the same way, and a Sunday School organization that encourages involvement in ministry.

An effective program of equipping students for ministry requires the entire Sunday School staff to work together as a team. It also needs the cooperation of the pastor and parents. As in other Sunday School ministry goals, teachers and leaders are instrumental in carrying out the program.

For a program of equipping students for Christian ministry to reach maximum productivity, three elements are vital: challenging students to greater faith, conveying enthusiasm, and emphasizing the need for further training.

## *For Further Discussion*

1. Discuss the pattern of how knowledge becomes behavior.
2. How can Sunday School teachers and leaders develop faithfulness?
3. Name some ways the Sunday School program can stress ministering for Christ in the students' world.
4. List some ways pastors are important to effectively equipping students for ministry.
5. How can parents influence their children to become involved in ministering for Christ?
6. What is the Sunday School leadership's role in carrying out the equipping ministry?
7. Give five sources of ideas for getting students involved in ministering for Christ in their world.
8. How can teachers challenge their students to demonstrate greater faith?
9. Why is enthusiasm so important to a productive equipping ministry?
10. Name some ways students can further their education in preparing to minister for Christ.

## *For Application*

1. Prepare an equipping program for your entire Sunday School or for a single class.
2. Design your own self-improvement program to help you become a better equipper of students to minister for Christ.

# SUNDAY SCHOOL MINISTRY GOALS

|  | EVANGELISM<br>Matthew 28:19,20 | EDIFICATION<br>Titus 2:7 | EQUIPPING<br>2 Timothy 2:2 |
|---|---|---|---|
| **Pastors** | Promote evangelism to the whole congregation<br>Contribute the evangelism model | Contribute to Bible study and spiritual growth counsel | Support and encourage the congregation by providing vision for ministry readiness |
| **Parents** | Alert to the readiness of their own children | Nurture their children in spiritual matters through example in the home | Participate with their children in active service |
| **Teachers** | Build rapport with their students | Develop personal friendships with students, leading to mutual spiritual discovery | Model Christian service |

# EVALUATION

## 5

Many people make an annual appointment with their doctor for a physical exam. The doctor carefully checks each of the many body systems and utilizes a number of tests to insure an accurate diagnosis of the patient's health. The purpose of such an exam is to determine the general level of health and to discover any small problems which, if left untreated, could turn into bigger problems. If any health concerns are uncovered, the doctor may prescribe medication or another course of treatment. The doctor will also offer a prognosis on what will likely happen if the suggested treatment is, or is not, followed. Most people do not enjoy the process of the exam itself, although they do understand its importance to maintain optimum health.

The Sunday School ministry in many local churches is in need of a similar check-up. Such an evaluation, like a physical exam, can provide a diagnosis of the current health as well as suggest ways the ministry can be improved.

### *Reasons for evaluation*

To receive the most help from an evaluation, it is important to understand the reasons why the process itself is important. Sometimes people will say, "I know I'm not feeling well, but I don't want to go to the doctor because I may discover that something is wrong with me." Of course, putting off the visit only delays the inevitable and the wait may make the situation worse. Sometimes church leaders may resist evaluating the Sunday School ministry because they fear discovery that something is not going well. Keep in mind, however, that evaluation itself only discovers problems that already exist, it does not create them. Evaluation, if properly done, is designed to help improve the overall quality of the ministry. There are two main reasons why evaluation is important; it is biblical and practical.

### Evaluation is biblical

Evaluation is a biblical concept. First, the New Testament encourages believers to evaluate themselves. In the context of preparing to celebrate the Lord's Table, Paul writes "A man ought to examine himself before he eats of the bread and drinks of the cup" (1 Cor. 11:28). This self-evaluation is important because if we do not accurately evaluate ourselves, we are in danger of being disciplined by God (1 Cor. 11:31-32). If it is important for Christians to evaluate themselves individually, it is logical to assume we should also be concerned about evaluating the ministries in which we are involved.

Second, we should be involved in evaluation because God is involved in constant assessment of us. Revelation 2 and 3 contains letters written from Jesus, through the apostle John, to seven churches in Asia Minor. These letters are essentially Jesus' evaluation of spiritual life in each church. Within each letter Jesus lists the strengths and weaknesses of the church and what was needed to improve the situation. The refrain in each letter "he who has an ear, let him hear what the Spirit says to the churches" (Rev. 2:7; 2:11; 2:17; 2:29; 3:6; 3:13; 3:22) underscores the importance of Jesus' evaluation. We should be aware that God is evaluating our church, just as He evaluated those seven churches.

Third, the New Testament teaches that every believer, after death, will be evaluated by God at a future event referred to in the New Testament as the "judgment seat of Christ" (2 Cor. 5:10). The purpose of this judgment is not to determine one's eternal destiny (that is determined in this life on the basis of trusting in Christ alone for salvation), but rather to evaluate our service to Christ since conversion. Paul writes that in light of this future event "we make it our goal to please him . . . for we must all appear before the judgment seat of Christ, that each one may receive what is due him for the things done while in the body, whether good or bad" (2 Cor. 5:9,10). Since we will one day give account to God for our actions, should we not be diligent in evaluating every ministry to make sure they are pleasing to God?

### Evaluation is practical

We should evaluate our church's Sunday School ministry because it works. A properly conducted evaluation is designed to help you determine the answers to these questions:

1. Where has our Sunday School ministry been in the past?
2. How is our Sunday School ministry organized?
3. What are the strengths and weaknesses at present?
4. How effective is the current Sunday School ministry?

5. How are workers being trained for the Sunday School?
6. Where is our Sunday School ministry going in the future?
7. What can be learned from this evaluation to help our church's Sunday School triumphantly face the future?

A well-done evaluation will make your Sunday School a more effective tool in fulfilling the Great Commission. Evaluation is not a magic solution for all your problems, but it is an excellent diagnostic tool to point you in the right direction.

Although evaluation can be done solely by people within your church (a pastor, leadership council, or Christian education board), it is often helpful to acquire the assistance of a trained Christian educator to help you interpret the results of your survey. An experienced Christian educator can also assist your church in implementing an action plan for improvment.

## Prerequisites to successful evaluation

The first prerequisite to success is that you believe evaluation is both necessary and desirable. If the evaluation is not confidently presented as the right thing to do, or if leaders withhold judgment as to its value until afterward, it is better not to do it.

Second, participants must strongly commit to being as objective as possible in the process. Sometimes it is difficult for long-term participants to clearly see what is actually happening. To prevent this, involve people in the process who have participated in Sunday School over varying periods of time.

Third, a properly done evaluation requires a commitment of time from those doing the analysis. There is no such thing as a microwave evaluation. Evaluation is hard, time-consuming work.

Fourth, it is absolutely critical for the church leadership to commit to a course of action on the evaluation results. If there is resistance to action, it is best not to do the evaluation at all. The whole purpose of the evaluation process is to address where your Sunday School ministry is now and how it can be improved.

Fifth, for an evaluation to be successful, the process must be supported by the senior pastor and the elder/deacon board *before* the process of evaluation begins. All leaders must be united for the evaluation process and resulting changes to be effective.

Finally, the entire process must be saturated with prayer for wisdom at each step. Evaluate because you desire to have the best Sunday School ministry possible for the glory of God.

## Procedure for successful evaluation

First, determine the evaluation time frame. Normally six weeks to three months is required, depending on the church size, availability of data, and the number of people involved in collecting the data.

Second, assign specific areas of the evaluation to one or more people. ETA has designed a *Sunday School Ministry Evaluation Form*[1] examining six areas: General Information/History, Leadership/Administration, Goals/Objectives, Recruitment/Training, Budget, and Facilities. There are subjective as well as objective areas of evaluation. The last part of this form, the Overall Evaluation of the Sunday School Ministry, will be completed collectively as reports are gathered for each of the six areas.

Third, differentiate between facts and opinions. For example, the average Sunday School attendance for the previous year is a fact, not an opinion. The vision of your leadership, however, is an opinion. Facts do not change. Opinions can change.

Fourth, focus on where things are, not where you would like them to be. If you know accurately where you are, you can more easily plot a course to get where you want to go. Admitting where you are does not mean that is where you want to stay.

Fifth, after all the data is gathered, the people in each area should answer the following questions:

   a. What is the greatest strength in this area of our program?
   b. What can be done to improve this area even more?
   c. What is the greatest weakness in this area?
   d. What can eliminate or minimize this weakness?
   e. What are the most important changes needed?
   f. What are the top three changes, in terms of priority, that need to be made in the next six to twelve months?

Sixth, after the individual areas of evaluation are completed, all involved in the process should review the results together.

Seventh, begin to develop an action plan based on your Overall Evaluation. The action plan consists of concrete steps needed as a result of what the evaluation discovered. After all action steps are listed, prioritize them. Then, a specific completion time should be assigned to each action step.

Eighth, present your evaluation with the action plan to the appropriate leadership responsible for the Sunday School ministry. Obviously, if some plans involve adding another Sunday School hour or expanding your building, the entire congregation (depending on your form of church government) may need to be involved.

Ninth, when approved by the proper authorities, implement your action plan, keeping to the projected time frame.

Finally, in eighteen to twenty-four months, repeat the evaluation process again. If a church is involved in an on-going process of evaluation, subsequent evaluations usually take less time. Regular evaluations of the Sunday School will help uncover and correct small problems before they turn into big problems.

---

[1] This form appears in this chapter in condensed form and is included in its entirety as a reproducible handout in the *Instructional Resource Package* available for this course.

## *Sunday School Ministry Evaluation Form*

### General Information/History

1.  What is the location of your church: inner city, suburbs, rural?
2.  What is the size of the town/city where your church is located?
3.  How many people live within a half-mile radius of your church? A mile-radius?
4.  When was your church founded?
5.  Is your church independent or part of a network? What is your current affiliation?
6.  What is your church's current active membership?
7.  Chart these statistics for the past five years: Average Sunday School attendance, average worship attendance, average Sunday evening attendance, average mid-week attendance. If your church is younger than five years old, go back as far as possible.
8.  Based on the above chart, our church is:
    \_\_\_\_ Doing Great!
    \_\_\_\_ Growing, but not as fast as we should
    \_\_\_\_ Some growth, but the growth rate is slowing
    \_\_\_\_ We're "holding our own"
    \_\_\_\_ Attendance is slipping
    \_\_\_\_ We are losing more than we are gaining
    \_\_\_\_ Historic low attendance
9.  If the trend indicated in the above chart continues another five years, what will your situation be?
10. Estimate the number of friends, relatives, and neighbors (those who are in driving distance of your church but do not currently attend any church) of your current attendees. This is your Sunday School's growth potential!

### Leadership/Administration

1.  Are there any paid staff people with leadership/administrative responsibilities in the Sunday School ministry?
2.  Do you have a board of Christian education in your church? If so, briefly describe its operation with the Sunday School.
3.  Do you have an organizational chart of the church's Sunday School program? If so, is it accurate? Is this chart available to all teachers and workers?
4.  Are ministry handbooks developed for each Sunday School department? These handbooks should include:
    —Outline of Program
    —Resources Available/Provided
    —Personnel/Ministry Descriptions
    —Logistics: Who, what, when, where, why?
    —Evaluation Form

5. Is there a regular meeting of Christian education teachers and workers? If so, when, how often, and what is the purpose of the meeting?
6. What curriculum materials are being used in each Sunday School department?
7. What is the procedure for selecting curriculum materials?
8. What percent of the Sunday School teachers use audio-visual aids in the classroom?
9. What types of audio-visual aids are available for use?
10. Who (person or a committee) correlates all of the curriculum materials that are used?
11. Does the church have a library? If so, list the types of materials that are available in it for use by teachers.
12. Does the Sunday School have a resource center? What supplies and equipment are available in the center?
13. What is the vision of your church's leadership for your church in the next year? Five years? Ten years?
14. What is the role of the Sunday School ministry in this vision?

### Goals/Objectives

1. What is the purpose statement of your church's Sunday School ministry?
2. What are the specific ministry goals that flow from the purpose statement?
3. What is the purpose statement for each of the departments (age groups) in your Sunday School?
4. Are your stated goals/objectives being met?
5. How do you track whether goals/objectives are being met?
6. How can your church's Sunday School ministry become more focused on the biblical goals of Christian education?
7. Is the Sunday School involved in the visitation of prospects and the follow-up of visitors? If not involved, how is follow-up taking place? If so, please explain.
8. Are teachers encouraged to be involved in the lives of their students? If so, what kinds of activities outside of class involve teachers in the lives of students?

### Recruitment/Training

1. Briefly outline the recruitment process your church follows in recruiting Sunday School teachers and workers.
2. Are the people who attend your church regularly surveyed to determine their experience in and availability for ministry?
3. Are courses/seminars offered on a regular basis which guide people to discern their spiritual gifts?

4. Are ministry descriptions available to recruiters for all positions?
5. Are Sunday School teachers required to be church members in good standing?
6. Are Sunday School teachers required to be in agreement with the church's doctrinal statement?
7. Do you have a training program for your teachers? If so, rate its effectiveness in these areas: Bible Content, Doctrine/Theology, Leadership Skills, Ministry Skills, Evangelism Skills.
8. Do you have a written agreement with Sunday School teachers and workers?
9. Do you have a process for evaluating church workers? If so, briefly describe it.

**Budget**
1. Based on your church's most recent budget, what are the top five priorities of your church?
2. In terms of percent of total budget dollars, where does the Sunday School program rank?
3. What is your Sunday School's per pupil/per week expenditure (include salaries, curriculum materials, building rental costs, etc.)?

**Facilities**
1. Determine the square footage of the entire church facility with breakdowns by room.
2. What percentage of square footage is auditorium/sanctuary space?
3. What percentage of square footage is educational space?
4. What space is available during Sunday School which is not being used currently for classrooms?
5. In your opinion, what classrooms are too small (in terms of students to square feet)? See the chart on page 77.
6. Which rooms could benefit from a new room arrangement?
7. Which rooms need redecorating?
8. Which rooms do not have the proper size tables and chairs?
9. What additional space would your church need if attendance grew annually by 5%? By 8%? By 10%?
10. Is there any off-site educational space available (e.g. meeting room of an apartment complex, school, private home of church member, etc.)?
11. How many parking spaces are available at your church: (a) off-steet paved, (b) off-street unpaved, (c) on-street paved?
12. What is the size of your church's land (in acres)?

13. What, if any, are future building plans for the church facility?

## Overall Evaluation of the Sunday School Ministry

1. In your opinion, what are the three greatest strengths of your church's Sunday School ministry? Are there ways to increase the impact of these strengths?

2. In your opinion, what are the three major weaknesses in your church's Sunday School ministry? Are there ways to minimize or correct them?

3. In your opinion, what are the three most important changes that need to be made in your church's Sunday School ministry?

4. In your opinion, what should be your church's top three priorities as it seeks to improve its Sunday School ministry in the future?

## Summary

Rank your church's Sunday School ministry in these key areas (10 being the best):

| Area | Our Sunday School is Currently Here |
|---|---|
| Leadership/Administration | 1 2 3 4 5 6 7 8 9 10 |
| Goals/Objectives | 1 2 3 4 5 6 7 8 9 10 |
| Recruitment/Training | 1 2 3 4 5 6 7 8 9 10 |
| Budget | 1 2 3 4 5 6 7 8 9 10 |
| Facilities | 1 2 3 4 5 6 7 8 9 10 |
| Overall Sunday School Ministry | 1 2 3 4 5 6 7 8 9 10 |

# ORGANIZING FOR ACTION

# 6

Good organization is vital to effectiveness. In a broad sense, Sunday School organization is a combination of necessary individuals, equipment, facilities, materials, and tools. When all these components are assembled in a systematic and effective way, Sunday School may then accomplish the objectives laid before it. All staff members need to recognize their responsibility to the Sunday School and function within the objectives of the ministry. They will also recognize the need to cooperate with individuals or groups outside the Sunday School. Viewing the Sunday School as an organization of interdependent members will raise the standards of the school in general and the quality of its leadership. Consequently, the ministry of teaching is elevated in the eyes of the church.

## *Benefits of organization*

Understanding the benefits of effective organization is essential to developing and implementing a Sunday School program. Sometimes people confuse organization with bureaucracy. Organization is more properly equated with terms such as *order* and *efficiency*. If we are to be effective in communicating the Word of God in the Sunday School, we must go about our task "in a fitting and orderly way" (1 Cor. 14:40). Organization brings many benefits to the Sunday School.

### Develops teamwork

In a successful sports team, all players must sacrifice their own desires for personal achievement and cooperate with their teammates. Star players alone cannot win at team games. All members must perform their specific roles in each play. So it is in Sunday School ministry. The united effort of all staff members produces far greater progress than the disconnected efforts of individuals.

### Identifies responsibilities

Unorganized Sunday Schools are usually ineffective. Organization makes it possible to clearly define responsibility, assign tasks, and indicate who is responsible for what and to whom.

### Provides for effective teaching

Preparation for God's service begins with foundational knowledge of God's Word. The Sunday School exists for teaching God's Word. Although it has other ministry functions, teaching that produces Word-centered students is the desired outcome. The first objective of organization is to create the proper environment for quality teaching. Organization does not create effective teaching but it does cultivate, enhance, and facilitate it. A well-organized Sunday School provides comfortable, adequate classroom space and uninterrupted teaching time. It encourages regular, punctual attendance.

### Clarifies God's overall purposes

Organization also helps define the functions and purposes of Sunday School as it relates to the church's total educational program. Disciplined workers learn to organize their efforts, in love, "to prepare God's people for works of service, so that the body of Christ may be built up until we all reach unity in the faith and in the knowledge of the Son of God and become mature, attaining to the whole measure of the fullness of Christ" (Eph. 4:12,13).

### Focuses the aims of teaching and learning

Organization gives aim, form, and drive to building an effective curriculum. Sunday School leaders must know what they believe. They must have evangelistic fervor and spiritual depth. Effective teachers and leaders know how to relate current issues to what the Bible says. The philosophy of church education must be clearly distinguished from every philosophy that denounces the authority of the Word of God. Organization helps teachers and leaders know what should be taught, why it is important, and how best to present it.

### Enlists all members' talents

Some church members contribute little or nothing in return service. The church must be organized to develop servants who serve! The Sunday School is the key workshop for achieving that goal.

The church needs leaders and each department in the Sunday School requires teachers and assistants. Modern expectations of the church afford limitless opportunities for ministry. Proper organization can manage the recruitment, orientation, and communication of positions best fitted to the talents, interests, and experience of church members. Organization gives people the opportunities to explore new fields of service that may differ from previous interest. Sunday School leads believers in discovery of potentials within themselves. Some followers develop into leaders. By creating an individual sense of belonging, organization serves as an important means to develop Christian character.

A church that equips its members to teach also develops their spiritual growth. Spiritual maturity makes a valuable impact on the community. The well-organized Sunday School can discover leaders, disciple students, and deepen the church's spiritual life.

### Encourages community outreach

Passively reminding participants to invite people to come to Sunday School is not usually an effective outreach into the community. Today's culture is conditioned for more assertive effort. An organized outreach program that recruits, equips, supervises, and evaluates those who are committed to community evangelism will bring new people into the fellowship. The very nature of Sunday School, with its emphasis on groupings and discipleship, offers a clearly identified starting place for an effective outreach program.

## *Personnel in organization*

Sunday School staffs include personnel organized in terms of administration, supervision, teaching, and supportive staff. Administration typically flows from a coordinating board or committee to a supervisor or director for the program. The chief decision makers are responsible for: determining aims, establishing policies, and giving general oversight in reaching objectives.

The aims of organization are realized through adequate supervision. Staff structure exists to make the teaching experience possible. Effective teaching will confront students with the truths of God's Word, lead them to a personal relationship with the Lord Jesus Christ, and ground them in their faith. Three spiritual gifts are helpful in Sunday School leadership.

### Administration—1 Corinthians 12:28

The word translated "administration" literally means to steer or guide a ship (this is its only appearance in the New Testament). It is one of the gifts of the Spirit and refers to the helmsman of a ship. The analogy is that a ship's owner decides where and when to sail and the helmsman charts the course and organizes the crew in order to sail the ship.

Administration is related to the Sunday School ministry in a similar way. The church's leadership determines policies and ministry goals while those with the gift of administration determine how to fulfill the policies and meet the goals.

### Evangelism—Ephesians 4:11

Not every Christian has the gift of evangelism but every Christian should witness. Sunday School is the principal ministry where children (during their formative years) and teenagers (in their most impressionable years) encounter evangelism efforts. The claims of Christ should be presented clearly in every Sunday School.

### Education—Romans 12:7

The Sunday School's educational effort is distinct from its administration. Though each complements the other, different personnel are needed for their respective tasks. Teachers are chosen for their gifts and abilities, professional training, and/or experience. Church education is concerned with the instructional standards that support and implement the curriculum, inspire teachers, and nurture students. The Sunday School, therefore, must cultivate a well-equipped and trained teaching staff.

In the common staff relationship, classroom teachers cooperate with a prescribed organizational structure to relay communications regarding their operational needs. Regardless of the model applied, all participants must keep in mind the ultimate objective is bringing people into Christlikeness.

## *Models of organization*

Contemporary Sunday Schools use a variety of models that are often subdivided to designate periods of life. The four main divisions are:

| | |
|---|---|
| Preschool | Birth through five years of age |
| Elementary | First through sixth grade |
| Youth | Seventh grade through high school graduation |
| Adults | College age and older |

The two traditional models for further division (or grading) are the *departmental model* and the *closely graded model*. Contemporary curriculum publishers use these units of grading that, in turn, are commonly adopted by local Sunday Schools.

### Departmental model
#### Traditional
#### Sunday School

| Departments | Grades | Ages |
|---|---|---|
| Nursery | | Birth–1 |
| Preschool | | 2–3 |
| Kindergarten | K-4, K-5 | 4–5 |
| Primary | 1–3 | 6–8 |

| | | |
|---|---|---|
| Junior | 4–6 | 9–11 |
| Junior High | 7–8 | 12–13 |
| or Middle School | 6–9 | 11–14 |
| Senior High | 9–12 | 14–17 |
| College/Career | | 18–24 |
| Adult | | 25 and over |

## Closely graded model

Clustering students by specific age and school grade is called *closely grading*. There is a distinct advantage for maintaining separate classes for young teenagers and older teenagers. Aside from the obvious socialization issues, the greatest number of students fall away from Sunday School between the ages of twelve and sixteen. During these impressionable years, good teachers, well-organized departments, and challenging curriculum materials must be provided.

Closely Graded Departments are:
   Infants (0-2 years; subdividing as needed)
   2 year olds
   3 year olds
   4 year olds (or K-4)
   5 year olds (or K-5)
   1st Grade
   2nd Grade
   3rd Grade
   4th Grade
   5th Grade
   6th Grade

Designations should complement the local school system if possible. Large churches, for example, may need a P-1 (pre-first) grade class. Post-elementary divisions may prefer to identify themselves with a designation for the youth ministry philosophy of the local church. Adults, accordingly, may vary in identification depending on the curriculum; either age-graded or topical studies.

## Elective model

A new problem in the contemporary Sunday School is adult dropout. This happens most commonly among newly-married young adults whose busy schedules and new responsibilities compete with earlier church loyalties. The church that wisely provides for adequate infant care and early childhood education will be especially attractive to young families. Likewise young, career-oriented adults and senior citizens have unique needs that will affect participation if left unattended. For this reason, many churches find *topical study electives* rather than age grouping to be effective for adults.

## Extension model

Some Sunday Schools will operate a traditional extension ministry in much the same way a school offers courses away from the main campus. Members who cannot attend regularly because of age, illness, home responsibility, employment, or other reasons should not be denied the benefits provided by the Sunday School. The support may be needed even more than if they were regular attenders. Shut-in members are also valuable prayer supporters.

## Structural projections

When organizing the Sunday School into departments, it may be necessary to carefully predict the enrollment of each. Conditions vary among communities. In one town, young children may dominate the population. In a college town, students and young professionals may be proportionately larger. Barring those anomalies, the general percentage of enrollment will look something like this:

| Department | Ages | Percent |
|---|---|---|
| Nursery | Birth–3 | 7 |
| Kindergarten | 4–5 | 8 |
| Primary | 6–8 | 10 |
| Junior | 9–11 | 10 |
| Junior high | 12–14 | 10 |
| Senior high | 15–17 | 10 |
| College/career | 18–24 | 10 |
| Adult | over 25 | 35 |

It is neither necessary nor desirable for the entire school to assemble for opening and/or closing exercises. The time is more efficiently spent within each department or grade conducting activities correlated with its lessons.

For the promotion of common interest and enthusiasm, the entire school might assemble for special days, such as a Missions Rally Day or Children's Emphasis Day. These occasions need not interfere with the Sunday School's educational program and may help to unify some goal of interest to the total church program.

## *Procedures for organization*

Continuous supervision is the mark of a well-organized Sunday School. To ensure good organization it is helpful to preserve departmental lines, require regular reports, and conduct staff meetings.

### Preserve departmental lines

Departments should not be combined once they are established. Young students should be promoted from one department to another as soon as they complete the required number of years or grades. As a general rule, teachers should not transfer from one department to another each year, but should focus on specializing in the age group for which they are best fitted.

### Require regular reports

No assignment should be made or task committed without provision for a report. Accountability is important. Staff members must know the definite times, places, and types of service they will be required to give. A deadline for completion dignifies a task and quickens its execution. To assign a task and then ignore it creates the impression that it is of little consequence.

### Conduct meaningful staff meetings

Effective organization is not possible without regular prayer and planning. Pray for spiritual power and wisdom. Plan for intelligent, effective effort. Regular training allows superintendents to communicate inspiration, information, and instruction.

## Summary

In order for Sunday School to be effective, good organization is vital. A well-organized Sunday School develops teamwork within its staff, identifies each person's responsibilities, provides for effective teaching, clarifies God's overall purposes, focuses the aim of teaching and learning, enlists all members' talents, and encourages community outreach.

A basic step in organizing the Sunday School is establishing divisions. Even in the smallest schools, at least four basic divisions are used: preschool, elementary, youth, and adult. Most schools subdivide these groups into smaller departments and grades in order to better meet the students' needs. A well-organized Sunday School of average size usually includes at least nine departments: nursery, preschool, kindergarten, primary, junior, junior high, senior high, college/career, and adult.

Three procedures that keep a Sunday School on the road to success are: effective departmental structure, requiring accountability from teachers and leaders, and regular meetings.

## For Further Discussion

1. Briefly define your Sunday School organization.
2. Name at least seven benefits derived from good organization.
3. How are each of these benefits evidenced?
4. Define staff-line relationships and show how they operate.
5. How effective are the basic divisions of the Sunday School?
6. Name nine departments of the Sunday School with their corresponding ages and grades.

## *For Application*

1.  Diagram your Sunday School organization showing the relationships of the administrators to the departmental leadership to the various departments and classes.

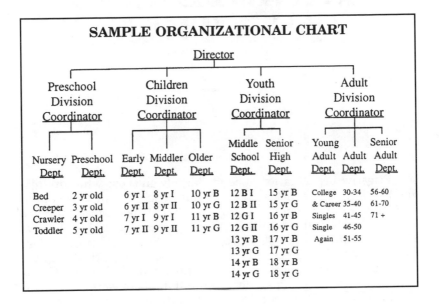

SAMPLE ORGANIZATIONAL CHART

Director

| Preschool Division Coordinator | Children Division Coordinator | Youth Division Coordinator | Adult Division Coordinator |
|---|---|---|---|

| Nursery Dept. | Preschool Dept. | Early Dept. | Middler Dept. | Older Dept. | Middle School Dept. | Senior High Dept. | Young Adult Dept. | Adult Dept. | Senior Adult Dept. |
|---|---|---|---|---|---|---|---|---|---|
| Bed | 2 yr old | 6 yr I | 8 yr I | 10 yr B | 12 B I | 15 yr B | College 30-34 | | 56-60 |
| Creeper | 3 yr old | 6 yr II | 8 yr II | 10 yr G | 12 B II | 15 yr G | & Career 35-40 | | 61-70 |
| Crawler | 4 yr old | 7 yr I | 9 yr I | 11 yr B | 12 G I | 16 yr B | Singles 41-45 | | 71 + |
| Toddler | 5 yr old | 7 yr II | 9 yr II | 11 yr G | 12 G II | 16 yr G | Single 46-50 | | |
| | | | | | 13 yr B | 17 yr B | Again 51-55 | | |
| | | | | | 13 yr G | 17 yr G | | | |
| | | | | | 14 yr B | 18 yr B | | | |
| | | | | | 14 yr G | 18 yr G | | | |

2.  After examining your Sunday School enrollment and attendance records, illustrate how departments and class grading can be expanded if additional members were brought into your program.

# MINISTERING AS A TEAM

# 7

Effective organization depends largely on those who administer its plans and policies. Leaders and teachers must be chosen carefully and trained thoroughly for their tasks. Most churches have a clearly defined policy, usually prescribed in their bylaws or denominational handbook, to govern the selection of leaders and teachers. If not, several basics are discussed in this chapter.

Often Sunday School leaders are appointed by a board of Christian education. This small decision-making body serves to mediate between Sunday School workers and the church's authority. This board examines the local church needs to determine specific methods and models used, observing some general guidelines. Specific terms of service, clear lines of authority and responsibility, and personal interaction are all essential issues.

## *Pastors*

Pastors function as the spiritual and inspirational head of the Sunday School. Some churches struggle to maintain unity of purpose in the total church program. Pastors are valuable in building the bridges between specific programs and leading the vision for Christian education. Pastors have responsibility in four areas: evangelism (providing appropriate process instruction), visitation (or personal interaction), teacher training (to exemplify excellence), and teacher installation (lending dignity and public endorsement to the ministry).

## *Christian education directors*

The educational ministries of a church must be under the

watchful administration of leaders who know God's Word and understand how to teach it in the church. If a Sunday School program is only one of many educational efforts, the Christian education director serves the purposes of coordination between the multiple efforts. He or she will be responsible for duties of:
—correlating curriculum to achieve balanced education;
—developing leadership potential;
—specializing in the functionality of the program;
—teaching whenever necessary;
—counseling the teaching staff;
—communicating information and vision about the program.
The director's vision and leadership is infectious because it focuses on reaching and teaching people for the Lord.

## *Superintendents*

Whenever the pastor or Christian education director are not available, a program superintendent becomes the indispensable administrator. Typically, Sunday School superintendents are not trained professionally for their tasks, but they can use their administrative talents for advancing and improving the teaching ministry.

Sunday School superintendents are, ideally, focused on this single ministry without the burdens of other offices or tasks. In addition to the basic spiritual qualifications expected of all church leaders, superintendents should be organized, proactive, assertive, enthusiastic, possess good people skills, and be efficient.

The superintendent's responsibilities are to direct all plans for enlarging and improving the Sunday School. Major issues include planning and execution of decisions, working with parents, delegating appropriate work through departmental leaders, and encouraging specific classes. Superintendents are great moderators when training sessions require planning and quality control.

Helpful resources are available for conducting meaningful staff meetings. Consult your local Christian education supplier or denominational headquarters for suggestions. Evangelical Training Association offers a complete meeting series for this purpose through its *Church Membership Program.*

As the managing administrator, a superintendent also provides sound financial planning for the operational expenses. This person usually performs the tasks of ordering curriculum materials and requisitioning additional space and equipment for teaching. This person may also be called upon to assist in planning a new educational building or devise other creative ways to carry out the teaching ministries.

Superintendents are often charged with assembling a support team of other contact people with expertise in areas that contribute to the teaching/learning environment.

There are six such support areas in a traditional Sunday school. These staff members should serve faithfully for the duration of their ministry assignment. Many smaller Sunday schools combine these responsibilities with other positions to alleviate the problem of additional recruiting. Nevertheless, the entire Sunday school team must be "God's fellow workers" (2 Cor. 6:1).

## Secretary/treasurers or clerical officers

This position requires the spiritual gift of helps and offers more sacrificial service and less public recognition than some other postions. Good clerical officers are characterized by an appreciation for details, neatness, and accuracy, with a genuine sense of value for permanent records and files. The major areas of responsibility for this position should be record keeping, correspondence and/or communication, and finances.

## Media center directors

Multimedia resources are increasing each year. Churches now frequently establish media centers to house electronic equipment, audio and video tapes, computer disks, and CDs. An efficient media center director coordinates these resources in much the same way a librarian monitors print materials.

Media center directors need a working knowledge of current multimedia teaching resources. They will find it exciting and adventuresome to investigate new products, research current trends, and keep themselves informed on future developments in this everexpanding field. Continuous contact with all Sunday school staff members will reveal their needs and desires. Most curriculum materials will print a list of equipment needs for each series of lessons. The media director should review the curriculum or otherwise establish means to identify suitable suggestions for these immediate requests.

It is always a comfort to teachers if the media director is trained in the field or, at least, knows how to operate the equipment in inventory. These centers rarely receive adequately funding if they are not included in the Sunday school or church budget. The amount needed can be augmented by personal contributions and special offerings.

If a new media center is being established, enlist the sympathetic cooperation of the church and its friends. The Sunday school might sponsor a media center "shower" by creating a wish list for potential donors. Again, a consultation with staff members is important to identify a wide variety of learning resources needed for all ages and interests—audio and video tapes, filmstrips, overhead transparencies, records, books, flannelgraphs, and teaching pictures. Distribute this list throughout the church membership suggesting each family select one item to contribute or find a friend to offer a donation to the new center. This should get the new media center off to a good start.

Media center directors must keep all staff members informed of the resources available and how to use them. Many teachers are not familiar with all the newest resources and techniques but would be willing to try them if they received some instruction on their use and availability.

Media center directors should be adequately authorized to acquire new resources for the centers and catalog these resources and supervise the scheduling of their use. To accomplish this, directors should enlist the active support of pastors, superintendents, and other leaders.

## Missions coordinator

Although education about missionaries and their fields of service should be carried on in all church educational programs, Sunday schools are usually more involved. For this reason, Sunday school staffs need coordinators to see that mission education is taking place in Sunday school classrooms. They also maintain current information about the missionaries and any projects the church supports. Since they are responsible for communicating church sponsorship, they should also be members of the church's missions committee and regularly propose events that are facilitated through the Sunday school; whether it be a class adoption of a missionary family or some other organized prayer support.

## Music coordinator

When used effectively, music helps build and maintain effective Sunday schools. Music coordinators must work with department leaders and teachers to provide their students with meaningful musical experiences. Although musical training and experiences are valuable assets, they are not necessities for serving as music coordinators. They should, however, at least have a knowledge of who is available with musical training. Their main responsibility is to see that coordinated music is carried out in Sunday school classrooms. This can be accomplished with the selection of graded hymnals and songbooks. An inventory of musical resources and equipment should be maintained. If music coordinators are also members of existing music committees for the worship functions, the sharing of instruments, personnel, and supplies are better served.

It is ideal for each department to have its own musician (pianist or guitarist) and a song leader.

## Departmental leaders

Similar to the duties of a general superintendent, departmental leaders are basically responsible for administrative duties; the difference being only one department is the focus. Departmental leaders are responsible for planning activities that best suit the specific age or grade and nurturing teachers in that department.

### *Departmental secretaries or assistants*

As churches continue to grow, lay leaders can feel overwhelmed with responsibilities unless some duties are shared. The primary responsibilities of the departmental secretary or assistant are to share the burden of leadership, maintain departmental student records, and assist with handling resources.

### *Summary*

Well-organized Sunday schools depend on models that carry out team goals. Functioning as a team is a good metaphor when defining the specific duties the Sunday school staff will perform. Designing a chart to visualize the key roles each member will play is an excellent way to reinforce the unity of purpose a Sunday school organization must achieve.

### *For Further Discussion*

1. List the qualifications and responsibilities of your Sunday school staff.
2. Outline your Sunday school's method for handling financial responsibilities.
3. Why is a basic plan essential when electing leaders?
4. How does selecting appropriate music contribute to Sunday school effectiveness?
5. What are the qualifications and responsibilities of music coordinators?
6. Name the qualifications and responsibilities of media center directors.
7. What is the function of a missions coordinator?
8. Compare the functions of departmental leaders to those of general superintendents.

### *For Application*

1. Prepare a brief handbook for Sunday school leaders including the qualifications and responsibilities of each leader and staff member and a personal checklist of activities in which they should be involved. See the chart on page 58.
2. Prepare your own program for establishing a media center in your church. Plan what materials should be included in a well-stocked media center and decide how these materials will be obtained.

# DEVELOPING A MINISTRY DESCRIPTION

What does this ministry position exist to do?

*This ministry position exists for the purpose of . . .*

Who does this ministry position report to?

*This ministry position reports to _____.*

Who is this ministry position responsible for?

*This ministry position is responsible for the following ministry positions:*

What resources are available to help this ministry position fulfill its purpose?

*There is $_____ per month budgeted for the expenses related to this position.*

What training will be provided to the person who is in this ministry position?

*Training will be provided (when and where) for this ministry position.*

What evaluation process will be used with this ministry position and when will it take place?

*This ministry position will be evaluated by _____ on _____ utilizing the attached evaluation form.*

# ROLES AND RESPONSIBILITIES
# OF SUNDAY SCHOOL LEADERS

| General Superintendent | Division Coordinator | Department Leader | Teacher |
|---|---|---|---|
| Guides leaders in planning, conducting, and evaluating their work | Guides department leaders in planning, conducting, and evaluating their work | Guides teachers in planning, conducting, and evaluating their work | Guides leaders in Bible study with Bible learning activities, etc. |
| Recruits needed leaders for the Sunday School | Recruits needed leaders for the division | Recruits needed leaders for the department | Refers possible leaders for the Sunday School to the department leader |
| Secures resources for the Sunday School | Defines resources needed for the division | Defines resources needed for the department | Defines resources needed for the class |
| Helps leaders set goals for the Sunday School work | Helps department leaders set goals for the work of the division | Helps teachers set goals for the work of the department | Helps learners set spiritual growth goals |
| Provides training for the leaders of the Sunday School | Provides training for the leaders in the division | Provides training for the leaders in the department | Takes advantage of the training provided for Sunday School leaders |
| Coordinates the creation of new classes and departments as needed | Creates classes and departments as needed in the division | Creates new classes as needed in the department | Builds class up to the maximum size so new classes can be formed |
| Coordinates the outreach program for the Sunday School | Coordinates the outreach program for the division | Coordinates the outreach program for the department | Cooperates in the outreach program for the department |
| Conducts planning meetings for the Sunday School | Conducts planning meetings for the division | Conducts planning meetings (monthly) for the department | Attends monthly planning meetings for the department |
| Communicates to leaders policies, procedures, and any changes in these | Communicates to department leaders policies, procedures, and changes in these | Communicates to teachers policies, procedures, and changes | Keeps informed on changes in policies and procedures |
| Coordinates with other church agencies for a total teaching ministry | Coordinates all the division activities for a total program approach | Coordinates department activities for a total teaching approach | Cooperates with other leaders in the department for a total teaching approach |

From *Your Sunday School Can Grow* by Lowell E. Brown and Bobbie Reed (Glendale, CA: Regal Books, 1974).

# EQUIPPING AND TRAINING THE TEAM

## 8

A proven method for building effective Sunday Schools lies in a well-planned, carefully-executed, long-range equipping and training program. No Sunday School can truly fulfill its purpose unless it has effective staff members and productive students. Equipping leaders and teachers for service and training them in the most up-to-date methods will accomplish both.

### *Why equipping and training?*

Equipping staff members for ministry, as contrasted with only training them, is a distinction many feel strongly deserves attention today. This perspective maintains *equipping* focuses on developing the person to serve the Lord, whereas *training* provides skills to fulfill specific jobs.

Before volunteers can shift their focus from that of filling vacancies in the church to that of serving for ministry, they will require intentional instruction on this perspective. The service-oriented concept involves the following distinctions:

*Equipping concentrates on the person, whereas training concentrates on the task.* Equipping is far more concerned with developing the person than what the person does. Equipping, therefore, will assist individuals in discovering who they are, what their spiritual gifts are, and what God's plan is for them.

*Equipping develops the individual's potential, whereas training develops proficiency.* Task proficiency is the goal of training, while equipping is far more concerned with what the individual is called to do for Christ.

*Equipping teaches problem solving, whereas training teaches technique.* Equipping is able to empower the believer to resolve

59

issues, adapt techniques, and modify approaches that go far beyond the current experience and ministry task. Equipping encourages learning transfer.

*Equipping makes things happen, whereas training keeps things happening.* The believer who has been developed individually and creatively will be much more entrepreneurial in sensing ministry needs and responding to them in personal ministry.

*Equipping initiates new ministry, whereas training generally maintains existing ministry.* Individually developed believers are more open and responsive to the Spirit's leading to fresh new challenges in their world.

*Equipping assures ministry future, whereas training perpetuates current conditions.* Equipped believers are more qualified to meet the challenges of change in society and community. To believers who have been equipped for ministry, changes are not seen as threats but as opportunities.

These distinctions between equipping and training are not intended in any way to discredit training at the expense of equipping. Rather, it is to demonstrate that the church needs both equipping and training. The more common model in the past, however, has been only that of training.[1]

## Understand the purposes and procedures

If the Sunday School's program of equipping and training is to be successful, it is necessary to have the end in sight before designing ways to achieve it.

### Purposes

Simply stated, the purpose for the equipping and training of educational staff is to improve teaching quality. Jesus equipping and training His disciples is the model.

One of the goals of the Sunday School should be to keep up with advances in the field of education. That is not to advocate chasing after fads and trends, but steadily and noticeably developing quality teaching in all departments. If new educational methods are not contradictory to the biblical basis for teaching, they may be worthy methods to adopt.

When an equipping and training program is properly carried out, other peripheral benefits will result. Students will be motivated to learn and numerical growth usually follows. A greater interest in evangelism and missions results when teachers and other staff members become involved with courses that require Word-centered study.

### Procedures

Most local church educational programs are effectively expedited by their own people—equipped and trained by their own leaders to do the educational task for the glory of God. A serious-minded believer, gifted by the Holy Spirit, can become a capable Sunday School teacher or leader. The salvation and spiritual growth of many people depend on the supply of trained teachers and other staff members to faithfully present the truth of God.

Equipping and training programs must be geared to the needs and resources of the local context. In some areas, churches find it necessary to develop their own program, but where possible, co-operation in a community training program can offer a wider exposure to classes and usually a higher level of instruction.

Equipping and training must be done—whether weekly, monthly, or annually, whether alone or in cooperation with other churches, whether on Sunday or during the week. It must be done. The larger questions frequently asked are, "How do I start?" and, more importantly, "How do I get people to respond?"

Starting equipping and training programs is usually sparked by leaders with vision who desire to revolutionize the church educational program. These leaders should be responsible for all phases of teacher development. They should encourage individuals to become involved. They should schedule in-service specialized departmental sessions and planning retreats for the entire educational staff. Teacher evaluation and student observation, as well as opportunities for guided teaching/learning, might also be under their direction.

Once the program is initiated and the concept of continuous preparation is accepted by the staff, scheduling the sessions can be determined. Churches with successful equipping and training programs have varied greatly in the number of courses and other events offered. All successful programs, however, seem to have one characteristic in common—they hold classes and other events as frequently as the total church calendar permits.

One pastor holds sessions for six consecutive evenings at the same time each year. Another sets aside twelve mid-week sessions for equipping new believers for ministry. Equipping courses are often presented as adult electives or during a Sunday evening program. Summer camps and Vacation Bible Schools often provide excellent opportunities. Unless programs are clearly and regularly scheduled, however, lasting effects are seldom obtained. Often the best time for equipping/training events is when they conveniently coordinate with other scheduled church activity.

**Use adequate materials**

An important ingredient in carrying out these programs is the quality of the instructional materials used. Better materials have never before been available for equipping and training church educational leaders and staff members. It is important to carefully examine the philosophy of preparation in materials for compatibility with your own church's goals.

## Denominational materials

Many large denominations have designed curriculum materials specifically geared to equipping and training educational leaders and teachers. Such programs usually focus on the particular denomination's theological and structural patterns and aim exclusively at helping people become better leaders and teachers in churches of that denomination.

## Non-denominational materials

Independent publishers of curriculum coordinate training materials to implement the specific items they publish. Again, compatibility is an important issue, but many training options are adaptable for any Christian education program.

## Evangelical Training Association (ETA)

ETA provides a uniquely-designed program for equipping and training church educational leaders and teachers for ministry. The Association publishes its own lay leadership curriculum, with assistance from its member school faculty. The curriculum is organized for use in several applications—traditional classrooms, seminars, staff meetings, multimedia presentations, and self-study.

The content of the courses designed for classroom use include Bible surveys, spiritual growth issues, human development, teaching methodology, Bible introduction, Bible doctrine, world missions, evangelism, and Christian educational program structure and administration. Each of these courses has a complete *Instructional Resource Package* that includes one copy of the text, an instructor's guide with reproducible worksheets, a set of transparency masters, and an audio or video cassette component. Additional resources include CD-ROMs and other enrichment items.

An optional incentive, known as *The Church Ministries Certificate Program*, rewards the adult student's progress with attractive certificates. Whether a small Sunday School ministry or ambitious Bible institute, flexibility for the individual ministry is ETA's strongest feature.

## *Use seminars, conventions, and conferences*

Seminars, conventions, and conferences continue to be used, however, some geographical regions find them a more popular option than others. They provide two very important ingredients in the overall leadership development process—inspiration and information.

## Seminars

Seminars are held by a variety of sponsoring groups. Often denominations will host district, regional, or national events for equipping and training local church educational leadership. Sometimes churches in a particular city or area join together to sponsor a team of church educational experts to conduct a weekend event for the same purpose. Church educational teachers and leaders are busy people so it becomes the task of the superintendent, assistant superintendent, or perhaps the minister or director of Christian education to recommend and/or structure an equipping and training program which will meet the staff's needs. Many local churches feel that sponsoring all of its educational staff at one seminar or convention each year is a wise investment.

## Conventions

The variety of church ministry and Sunday School conventions run from one-day events to multi-day events. Some attract less than a hundred people while others register several thousands. The general sessions usually feature speakers who can inspire teachers and leaders with the importance of their ministry; while workshop leaders provide practical help in new methodology and equipment. Attractive exhibits and helpful representatives offer opportunities to see the newest resources available and discuss programming possibilities.

## Staff meetings

Regular staff meetings are the single most important resource available to Sunday School leadership for their developing staff. What this group prays about, plans for, and implements will determine success and overall effectiveness. All Sunday School leaders, teachers, and other staff members should attend.

## Age-specific conferences

As often as necessary the superintendent should meet with the departmental leaders. They should present, explain, and promote the general policies, overall program, and the special emphases of their departments. Actions by the Christian education board can be studied and implemented. Effective conferences or retreats where plans and problems are discussed together provide for a healthy interchange of ideas. This cooperative endeavor will help the whole Sunday School function more smoothly, efficiently, and progressively.

## Leadership conferences

The Christian education leadership committee or board, which usually consists of key decision makers, should confer regularly. The Sunday School committee differs from the board of Christian education because of its singular focus. The board of Christian education concentrates on the entire church educational program—the Sunday School as well as other programs.

## Summary

Equipping and training educational staff promotes effective Sunday Schools. When teachers and leaders are equipped and trained for ministry, learning improves.

Although the main purpose in equipping and training educational staff is to improve the quality of education, many times additional benefits result. Among these are: elevation of student motivation, growth in attendance, and greater interest in evangelism and missions.

How churches equip and train their staff varies according to their size, denominational affiliation, and location. Some carry on programs throughout the year, others through concentrated, limited-period institutes. Some cooperate with other churches while others prefer to handle their own program. Whatever the format or schedule—equipping and training must be done.

Selecting the best resources to accomplish equipping and training goals helps promote effective programs. Many denominations publish materials for their own churches, but an increasing number of churches prefer those which cross denominational lines and emphasize basic ministry principles.

Although holding equipping and training classes within the local church probably constitutes the most effective approach, other less-formal structures and resources are available. These include seminars, Sunday School and church ministry conventions, monthly staff meetings, departmental superintendents' conferences, and Sunday School committee meetings.

## For Further Discussion

1.  Why is teacher equipping and training important in the local church?
2.  What are some of the distinctions between equipping and training?
3.  What is your church presently doing to develop leadership in its various educational programs?
4.  What type of format in terms of time, length, and emphasis would be most useful for your particular church?
5.  How could your church go about starting an equipping and training program?
6.  What is the major purpose of the staff meeting in the local church?
7.  What is your church presently doing about Sunday School and church ministry conventions? What else could it do?

## *For Application*

1. Set up plans for an educational staff equipping and training program in your church including methods for advertising it and enrolling your own leaders, teachers, and prospective teachers.
2. Prepare a list of the regional or local conventions or leadership clinics which are available to your staff. Begin to lay plans for encouraging attendance at these programs.
3. If you have had teaching experience, list areas of teaching where you feel you need definite help. Prepare a bibliography and/or other means which can help in answering your questions.
4. List outside speakers whose areas of specialization will most benefit your equipping and training program.

### *Notes*

1. Taken from *Christian Education: Foundations for the Future*, ed., Clark, Johnson, Sloat. Copyright 1991. Moody Bible Institute of Chicago. Moody Press. Used by permission. Patterson, Richard, "Equipping the Education Staff," 485-486.

# MINISTRY RESOURCES

# 9

Following the teaching staff, curriculum is the most important factor that affects learning. Curriculum includes the subjects taught, their interrelationship, sequence, and development of the total learning experience. Good teachers, using a good curriculum design, create high caliber Sunday Schools. For churches that accept the Bible as the center of the curriculum in their educational programs, all the goals, materials, and activities must be built on the Word of God. God's Word must be continually applied to all age levels on the basis of current needs and problems.

## *Curriculum philosophy*

Christian educators use the term *curriculum* in two ways. One includes the materials used, the learning processes and experiences of the student, and the teacher's philosophy and methods. The second usage refers to the materials used to implement the goals of the larger curriculum design. In this chapter the term *curriculum* will be limited to the second usage which leads to and accomplishes the basic aims of the Sunday School.

Curriculum designs prescribe the outline of studies for a particular age group serving a particular purpose. It is a means to an end, not an end in itself. Curriculum guides the students to accomplish educational objectives.

### Function of curriculum materials

The materials used must implement the curriculum and bring understanding to the students' learning experiences. Teachers' textbooks, students' study guides, visual resources, supplementary Scriptures, memory verses, and methods—all are defined as curriculum materials. Curriculum materials include information, activities, and experiences specifically related to areas common to an age group. Because life is complex and each person must deal with it realistically, curriculum materials must embrace the home, church, school, community, vocation, recreation, and all other related areas. Select curriculum materials which include a well-balanced program appropriate to changing maturity levels.

Teachers who use supplementary resources will more effectively assist their students with new information and guide their experience through:
— discussions and interviews;
— map studies, graphs, tables, globes;
— reading books, magazines, pamphlets;
— using mass media.

### Selecting curriculum materials

Someone in each Sunday School must be responsible for deciding what curriculum materials are used. The church must be sure that its curriculum is sound and effective and that the materials are in accord with its educational principles and policies. Denominational affiliation, the local church situation, particular community needs, and other factors may influence the decision.

The board of Christian education is the logical group to select curriculum materials. In some cases, the pastor or Sunday School superintendent make the decision. Before curriculum decisions are made, however, it is important to get input from the department leaders and teachers who will ultimately be using it in the classroom.

When selecting curriculum materials, it is wise to use a theologically-unified, correlated program through all age levels of the Sunday School. When the same curriculum is used in all age levels, broader Bible coverage results, lesson duplication is avoided, and families can discuss Sunday School themes more efficiently.

Sometimes it is determined that the educational objectives of the local church are better served by using more than one publisher. If this becomes necessary, avoid subdividing the program beyond the broader age categories of early childhood, elementary, teens, and adults.

When evaluating curriculum, answering questions like the list below helps the authorized person, committee, board, or group, with an informed decision.

*Content*
Is the material properly graded to the students' age-level, learning capacity, experience, interests, and needs?
Do the theological emphases agree with your denominational or local church's doctrinal statement?

Will it lead to growth in the areas of Christian experience, maturity, and practice?

Does it correlate with the church's overall Christian education program?

Is any handwork specifically related to lesson content and students' interests?

*Appearance*

Are the materials attractive and colorful?

Are Bible references clearly identified?

Does it encourage active Bible study?

Do the Bible and life-related stories capture students' attention?

Is all the copy clearly written?

Are they clearly printed and durably bound?

Are its costs within the Sunday School's budget?

*Learning Aids*

Does it provide a separate book, leaflet, or activity sheet for each student?

Is everything provided for teachers to present the entire lesson?

Are lesson aims clearly written, measurable, and attainable?

Is there a plan or an outline for lesson preparation?

Are lesson plans clearly explained and easily followed?

Are supplemental learning resources suggested such as maps, charts, tables, murals, posters, recordings, filmstrips, slides, videotapes, models, flannelgraphs?

Does it provide activities which capture students' attention at the point of contact?

*Application*

Are lessons related to previous and subsequent studies?

Are age-level appropriate, student-centered learning activities used such as buzz groups, brainstorming, story writing, reports, role plays, pantomime, projects, and drama?

Does it encourage students to discover answers themselves?

Are there methods for applying the lesson to life situations?

Are suggestions given for how students can respond to the lesson truth?

Are home assignments recommended?

*Enrichment*

Is there a bibliography of additional resources?

Are there helps for creating bulletin boards, displays, and illustrations?

Does it motivate students to attend church services and accept responsibilities?

Are good citizenship, community responsibility, honesty, ethics, and good morals stressed?

Are holidays and seasons celebrated?

# *Curriculum design*

What lies behind the curriculum materials used in Sunday School? Thousands of Sunday Schools will distribute new materials at the beginning of the next quarter. Hundreds of thousands of students and their teachers will use these materials as study guides. The printed page will make its impact on Sunday Schools around the world. Few Sunday School leaders and teachers have ever analyzed the philosophies and policies behind these curriculum materials.

The Comparative Curriculum Chart found on pages 70 and 71 supplies information about various types of curriculums. Based on questionnaires sent to several denominational and independent publishing houses, it presents a broad view of three different types of curriculum—uniform, departmentally graded, and closely graded. The chart is only a guide. It is not intended to suggest which type of curriculum should be chosen. Studying this chart will assist in evaluating the methods and contents of each type. It will also help you relate them to your church's educational principles and policies.

# *Curriculum adaptation*

Since adults comprise a wider and more diverse age group than ever before, special attention must be given to adult Christian education. Courses designed for men and women should relate the Scriptures to the specific problems of adult stages and their corresponding social issues. Some specialty areas to keep in mind when designing a well-rounded curriculum might be leadership training, Bible study, and various elective subjects.

## Leadership training

Optional courses that concentrate on leadership training in the adult Sunday School offer a challenge to prospective volunteers. All adults should be equipped and trained to study the Bible for themselves and to present its message to others. They should know how to challenge students, how to understand them, and what to expect from them. Adults thus equipped and trained will be inspired, qualified, and confident to serve effectively in the total church program.

## Bible study courses

Though every effort should be made to encourage adults to take an active part in Sunday School, some men and women will be interested only to the extent of attending an adult class that meets a present life need of their own. For this reason, many churches have offered ETA's Bible survey courses to address the growing biblical illiteracy. With this approach, adults broaden their overall understanding of the Bible and then concentrate on expanding their knowledge and experience by studying selected Bible

# COMPARATIVE CURRICULUM CHART

| | UNIFORM | DEPARTMENTALLY GRADED | CLOSELY GRADED |
|---|---|---|---|
| **Definition** | A course of study using the same Sunday school lesson for all students. | A course of study arranged so that all students within the same department study the same Sunday school lesson. | A course of Sunday school lessons for use with students who are graded by one age or one public school grade. |
| **Number of lessons taught each week** | One lesson is provided for the entire Sunday school, usually graded by departments. | One lesson is provided for each department. | One lesson is provided for each school grade or age level. |
| **Departments** | Cradle Roll, Nursery, Kindergarten, Primary, Junior, Junior High, Senior High, College and Career, Adult | | |
| **Teaching staff required** | One regular teacher required for each class. In some age groups, associate teachers and helpers may be of regular assistance. | | |
| **Assistant (substitute) teachers required** | Prepared assistants teach in any department, adapting content and method to age level. | Prepared assistants may teach in any class within a given department. | Essential to have at least one assistant teacher for each grade. |
| **Number of years in each cycle of lessons** | The cycle ranges from five to eight years, depending on the curriculum planning committee. | The cycle varies with curriculums, usually the same as the number of years included in the department. | One year cycle of lessons is used for each school grade or age level. |
| **Special emphases** | Depending on policy of the publisher, evangelism, missions, family life, temperance, stewardship generally are included. Dated lessons may stress seasonal emphases such as Christmas, Easter, Mother's Day, patriotic holidays. Undated lessons included auxiliary seasonal and holiday themes. Many courses are available for worthwhile elective studies. | | |

| | | | |
|---|---|---|---|
| **Bible coverage** | Approximately 35% to 50% of the Bible is included in each complete cycle and repeated in the next cycle. | A higher percentage of Bible usually covered. Some portions are repeated with a different emphasis, depending on age and characteristics of students. | |
| **Teaching aids** | Research materials include annual commentaries, teacher's weeklies, monthlies, and quarterlies. | The teacher's manual usually includes teaching aids and ideas, Bible study helps, background material, illustrations, suggestions for activities. | |
| **Correlation of worship and class session** | If worship periods are geared to any one age level, participation by others may be reduced. | Worship period is generally correlated with lesson theme and class session by departments. | Correlation of worship period and lesson theme is possible within each grade. |
| **Aims and objectives** | The curriculum should implement the Sunday school's total educational program by providing a course of study to help the students learn, understand, believe, and practice the message of the Bible. | | |
| **Extra-biblical materials** | Editors and publishers usually provide illustrative and explanatory material to help both teachers and students. These include geography, history, archaeology, science, customs, current events. | | |
| **Major educational principles** | One lesson adapted to the comprehension and understanding of each age group. | Lessons are graded by departments, combining 2 or 3 ages or school grades, gearing each to the understanding and experience of students. | Grading is by age or school grade, based on year-to-year change of needs, capacities, and abilities. |
| **Learning aids** | Lesson helps suggest a wide variety of projected and non-projected visual and audio aids. They are usually correlated with the lesson. Additional materials may be adapted. | | |
| **Student's study helps** | Students' manuals, workbooks, and take-home papers are basic. Additional aids include handcraft, Bible puzzles, questions, home study manuals, projects, and other expressional activities. May also provide examinations, tests, and other measurements of progress. | | |

books. Other needs may include doctrinal studies, biblical counseling, or spiritual growth issues.

**Elective courses**

Interest in elective courses is a popular approach. The decision to use elective courses with youth classes will depend largely on the teachers' leadership ability and the students' specific needs. Presently, several publishing companies produce excellent elective materials to use as quarterly studies. Topics include doctrine, personal evangelism, church history, non-Christian religions, leadership development, the Bible and science, Christian ethics, and a wide variety of other practical subjects. Such courses provide excellent teaching situations because students, whether youth or adult, enroll on the basis of personal interest. These courses also motivate teachers because they can teach courses that are of special interest to them or address stage-of-life concerns. A word of caution is to not sacrifice an entire adult program to elective studies without some options available to view the whole of Scripture. Elective study diets can rapidly become spiritual fast food.

## *Summary*

Next to the teachers themselves, the curriculum they use is the most important factor affecting classroom learning. Hence, choosing curriculum materials is very important.

When making curriculum choices for a Sunday School, be sure that the curriculum's philosophy is compatible with your denominational doctrine, your church's constituency, and the abilities of your teaching staff and student body.

With the rising adult population, Sunday Schools should consider providing maximum ministry to this expanding age group. Most contemporary Sunday Schools are providing an elective program for their adults as well as older youth. Classes that might be offered in this type of structure include: leadership training, indepth Bible study, personal evangelism, doctrinal studies, church history, Christian ethics, and other practical living subjects.

## *For Further Discussion*

1. Distinguish between *curriculum* and *curriculum materials* as used in this chapter.
2. How does the function of the curriculum differ from the function of curriculum materials?
3. What person(s) should select curriculum and curriculum materials?
4. What basic criteria should be considered when evaluating curriculum materials?
5. What educational helps for the student should be included in good curriculum materials?

## For Application
Order sample curriculum materials from various publishers to evaluate using the criteria in this chapter.

## Major Curriculum Publishers

Augsburg Fortress
PO Box 1209
Minneapolis, MN 55440
800-328-4648
FAX 612-330-3455

CharismaLife Publishers
600 Rinehart Rd.
Lake Mary, FL 32746
800-451-4598
FAX 407-333-7100

Concordia Publishing House
3558 S. Jefferson Ave.
St. Louis, MO 63118
800-325-3040
FAX 314-268-1329

Cook Church Ministries
4050 Lee Vance View
Colorado Springs, CO 80918
800-323-7543
FAX 719-536-3265

Gospel Light Publishing Co.
2300 Knoll Ave.
Ventura, CA 93006
800-446-7735
FAX 800-860-3109

Group Publishing
1515 Cascade Ave.
Loveland, CO 80538
800-447-1070
FAX 970-679-4373

National Baptist Publishing
6717 Centennial Blvd.
Nashville, TN 37209-1049
800-357-1874
FAX 615-350-9018

Scripture Press
4050 Lee Vance View
Colorado Springs, CO 80918
800-323-9409
FAX 800-430-0726

Standard Publishing Co.
8121 Hamilton Ave.
Cincinnati, OH 45231
800-543-1353
FAX 513-931-0904

Through the Bible Publications
1133 Riverside Ave.
Fort Collins, CO 80524
800-284-0158
FAX 970-495-6700

Union Gospel Press
PO Box 6059
Cleveland, OH 44101
800-638-9988
FAX 216-749-2205

Urban Ministries, Inc.
1551 W. Regency Ct.
Calumet City, IL 60409
800-860-8642
FAX 708-868-7105

# YOUR FACILITY AND MINISTRY

## *10*

The issues involved in determining church building design continue to change drastically and occasionally become an issue of controversy. As a result, churches find it difficult to make long-range plans for new educational facilities that house all their programs and other ministries.

The concept of long-range planning has always been crucial in designing facilities for churches. Careful planning is a stressful concern to congregations who experience rapid growth because they must create new classrooms, add to the present structure, or completely rebuild quickly.

Key words when planning to build are: needs, purpose, design, and function. These, in turn, produce another key word— *ministry*. All churches and Sunday Schools are interested in ministry. Buildings are adequate and satisfactory only if they enhance the ministry that God's people are called to render.

### *Needs and purposes determine design*

Two questions immediately surface: "What are the needs and purposes of the congregation now and what are they expected to be in future years?"

### Remodeling present facilities

By developing an overall plan of your facility on paper, a better focus on facility use is achieved without tearing down walls. It will be immediately visible whether inequities in needs exist. To best accommodate a variety of groups meeting in shared areas of the building, confer with other leaders to re-examine each group's needs.

Sometimes heavy drapery materials can be used as an alternative to accordion or folding walls. These materials may be pleated and made in double thickness for increased sound absorption. Draperies cost less than accordion walls and, when hung on proper tracks, serve the same purpose. Often adding acoustical ceilings and carpeting can also help absorb sound.

### Adding to existing buildings

In some cases new additions are very practical. Many older church buildings were constructed with high side walls so that a two-level educational wing could be added and not be above the roof line of the existing structure. A balcony or closed second-story space can often be installed at the rear of the sanctuary, with nursery facilities or classroom space below it.

When extensive remodeling is needed, it can be expensive. The cost per square foot is often higher than a new building and the facilities may soon become crowded again. Talking with architects, contractors, or building consultants is always necessary before considering an extensive addition. Preparing a master plan that includes projected educational needs will assure greater economy and fulfillment of purpose.

Churches with immediate educational space needs are understandably reluctant to add onto their existing structure. Purchasing and converting a nearby house or other building may be an option. Then, if conditions or situations change, the house or building could be sold—sometimes at a profit. Renting or leasing portable structures is also an attractive option for immediate use.

### Planning a new building

It cannot be emphasized too strongly that building plans are dependent upon the needs and purposes of the church *educational* ministry. If the church is serious about fulfilling Christ's Great Commission, buildings that house its educational program must take priority over athletic, social, and other program needs. Education nurtures all the other programs and cannot be sacrificed.

Good architects, designers, consultants, and/or engineers understand the needs of evangelical churches and are valuable resource personnel. They should be thoroughly familiar with the church's functional needs, know their craft, and be aware of the financial limitations. Find people with reputations for thoroughness, integrity, and willingness to economize—people who will provide what is really needed. Ask for and follow up on references. Visit a project they have recently completed. True professionals will not be offended by such requests.

Architects, however, cannot be expected to know the needs of every church. The building committee must formulate these and provide complete information for the architect who then translates them into sound building plans. Work for simplicity; always keeping in mind possible future expansion.

## *Design determines function*

The old question of which comes first, form or function, is as practical as it is philosophical. In reality, of course, the first step to be determined is the function of the educational program by clearly and specifically identifying its needs and purposes. Once these have been determined, the building can be designed.

If the Sunday School is divided into grades and departments, housing must include both departmental and individual classroom areas. These requirements vary greatly, depending upon the age of the students. See the chart on page 77 for more information.

### Design for the future

In some situations, crowded facilities can indicate that visitors are unwelcome. Attractive facilities appeal to the surrounding community. Sunday Schools that demonstrate little vision when a new building is erected often find their facilities overtaxed from the start. Remember that your facility makes a theological statement. It is wise to provide considerably more space than is necessary for the present enrollment. Carefully examine your rate of growth to project increases intelligently. Be sure to get a draft or blueprint so that the plans will not be forgotten.

### Design to conserve space

In estimating space requirements for Sunday School facilities allocate approximately 25 square feet per child and 10-12 square feet per young person and adult. Under normal conditions, nearly equal spaces can be allotted to the various children and youth departments. For example:
- Preschoolers will need their allotted square footage for more furniture, play areas, and learning centers.
- Elementary children will need their allotted space for more active learning activities.
- Teens will use their allotted square footage for breakout activities and social functions.
- Adults will need their allotted space for elective programming.

### Design for adequate departmentalization

Information on space requirements may seem irrelevant to the new or small Sunday School, especially if they do not have separate rooms for departmental groupings. A basement fellowship room or Sunday School auditorium may be used for children through the sixth grade (11 years old). Junior highs through adults may meet in the church sanctuary or auditorium. If more rooms

# DETERMINING SPACE IN AGE-DIVISION ROOMS

| Division | Age | For Each Department | | For Each Class | | Suggested Floor Space per Person | | | |
|---|---|---|---|---|---|---|---|---|---|
| | | Maximum Enrollment | Anticipated Attendance Capacity[a] | Maximum Enrollment | Anticipated Attendance Capacity[a] | Department Room[b] Minimum[b] | Department Room Recommended | Classroom Minimum | Classroom Recommended |
| Preschool | Birth–1 | 12 | 9 | Not Applicable | | 20 sq. ft. | 35 sq. ft.[c] | None | None |
| | Toddlers | 12 | 9 | | | | | | |
| | 2 | 15 | 12 | | | | | | |
| | 3 | 20 | 16 | | | No Preschool room smaller than 12x16[d] | | | |
| | 4 | 20 | 16 | | | | | | |
| | 5 | 20 | 16 | | | | | | |
| Children | 6,7,8 | 30 | 24 | Not Applicable[e] | | 20 sq. ft. 20x24[d] | 25 sq. ft. 25x30[d] | None | None |
| | 9,10,11[e] | | | | | | | | |
| Youth | 12–17 | 60 | 28–42 | 15 | 7–10 | 8 sq. ft.[f] | 10 sq. ft. | 10 sq. ft. | 12 sq. ft.[f] |
| Adult | 18–up | 125 | 56–87 | 25 | 11–17 | 8 sq. ft. | 10 sq. ft. | 10 sq. ft. | 12 sq. ft. |

Space is provided for each person expected to be in the rooms of the building. Determining the number for which to plan is the result of analyzing the projected enrollment, organization, and attendance.

In determining the total number of square feet of educational space required, the church should add to the floor space mentioned in the chart additional spaces for offices, corridors, stairways, rest rooms, storage, service space, and other accessory areas. A total of 35 to 50 square feet per person will be needed.

a. Average attendance may range from 45 percent to 70 percent of enrollment, depending on the age group and/or the community involved. In preschool and children's departments, provision should be made on the basis of 80 percent of enrollment in attendance. For youth and adults 70 percent of enrollment should be adequate.

b. Minimum space footage may be necessary in smaller churches, first units, or mission buildings.

c. Thirty-five square feet is considered as ideal. For churches planning to provide day care, kindergarten, and elementary school programs, at least 35 square feet will be required.

d. For rationale, consult the "Basic" books for the respective age divisions.

e. Existing assembly-classroom type facilities may be used for Children's departments. Additional tables, chairs, and chalkboards may be needed.

f. If open-room space is planned for youth, 13–22 square feet per person will be needed.

## SUNDAY SCHOOL SPACE STUDY

Room Number _____

This room contains _____ square feet of space.

This room is presently used by _____ (Class/department — age range — teacher).

The average attendance in this room during the last six months was _____

If used by *Adults* the room is adequate for _____ persons.

If used by *Youth* the room is adequate for _____ persons.

If used by *Children* the room is adequate for _____ persons.

If used by *Preschoolers* the room is adequate for _____ persons.

From *Building on Basics of Church Growth* (Herrin, IL: Leon Kilbreth Evangelistic Association).

are available, separate the school-age and preschool children, then the youth and adults. As enrollment and facilities enlarge, continue to subdivide each age group to increase teaching/learning effectiveness.

Various age and interest groups within the adult department may suggest entirely different curriculum and lesson presentation needs.

## *Function determines ministry*

What can be done in the buildings is simply another way of defining church and Sunday School ministry. The process is a cycle—study the present ministry to determine if it is meeting needs and fulfilling objectives; reinterpret needs and revise objectives for the future; decide on design for additional facilities which will determine function and thereby activate a new approach to ministry. To be sure, designing new facilities for maximum flexibility in function is a wise choice.

### Ministry to children

Plans should be made to have sufficient room for expanding nursery and preschool departments. Then endeavor to attract as many young families from the community as possible. When well-organized nursery and preschool departments are available, parents will feel free to bring their young children and will also stay themselves. Thus, the early provision for infants and preschoolers becomes an effective outreach to entire families. They are the nucleus of a great future church—a potential corps of Christian leaders.

In nursery and preschool departments, learning is often centered on familiar relationships. Children of this age need to be comfortable in small groups for expressional activity following the lesson presentation.

In the early elementary years, group interaction exists with class instruction. Designated classroom space is important to older elementary children. The size of classes in elementary years should generally be limited to eight to twelve students per teacher.

### Ministry to youth

Specialization with youth ministry now requires a designated space for their unique needs. Your church's philosophy toward youth ministry will dictate the type of space required; oriented toward athletic, musical, fellowship, or other emphasis.

### Ministry to adults

All demographic studies show the population is aging and the number of middle and senior adults will soon be greater than ever before. Significant implications in planning for adult education will result. For example, facility design should include fewer stairs, wider doorways, and wheelchair-accessible restroom facilities.

A renewed emphasis on small groups for fellowship and Bible study suggests not only separate, smaller rooms but also informal surroundings. One of the key factors in design is multipurpose planning—using one space for as many activities as possible.

In spite of the rising cost for housing and equipping today's Sunday Schools, building can be done economically with the help of modern functional architecture. Planning ahead is imperative. Spur-of-the-moment decisions cost much more and usually result in dissatisfaction. Take time to check and recheck needs. Spend time in prayer. Decide on the right architect or engineer. Visit other churches to study their facilities and use of materials. Confidently approach new construction with a prepared master plan that covers the total church program's needs.

## *Summary*

In order to provide the best possible educational program in the Sunday School, many churches find it necessary to build completely new buildings or significantly remodel their present facilities. But before doing either, churches should consider their needs, purposes, designs, and functions—or in a word—ministry.

When planning a building project, a congregation should ask itself, "What are our needs and purposes now and what do we expect them to be in the future?" Once the answers to these questions have been thoroughly considered, building plans can begin. At this point, a decision must be made whether to remodel the present facility, add onto the existing building, acquire a nearby building, or plan a completely new structure.

When designing a significant building project, it is important to design for the future, design to conserve space, and design for adequate departmentalization.

A church's building should be built to carry out its ministry. Space should be provided for the various age groups according to the number of people in the group and the kind of activities carried on within the group's program.

Recent studies show that the population structure is changing. Before deciding to build, be sure to study the demographics of the church, the community, and the surrounding area. Keep all this data in mind when planning church buildings.

For Sunday Schools needing more or better facilities—something can be done. Even in poor economic times, God's people can work together to provide adequate facilities in which to study God's Word. But before launching out into a building program, carefully evaluate your present needs, realistically plan for future growth, and fervently pray for guidance.

## For Further Discussion

1. How do the educational program's purposes and needs affect building design?
2. What are two major principles to keep in mind in conserving space?
3. What is standard procedure in determining space requirements for Sunday School facilities?
4. List various ways in which a building can be remodeled.
5. What qualifications should describe a designer, consultant, or engineer employed to help plan a new church building?
6. What is the best location for the church's educational unit?
7. What are the suggested class sizes in the various departments?
8. What are the advantages of having separate classrooms?
9. How do changes in demographics affect planning educational facilities?

## For Application

Though you may not be a member of the building committee, you will be a better Sunday School leader, teacher, or staff member if you know the facilities that are available in your building. The following chart will provide a helpful class project.

1. **General information**
   Sunday School enrollment _____
   Sanctuary (auditorium) capacity _____
   Number of classrooms _____
   Future enrollment possibilities _____
   Average attendance _____
   Church attendance _____
   Total capacity _____

2. **Specific information**

| | Yes | No |
|---|---|---|
| Are there enough classrooms? | \_\_\_\_ | \_\_\_\_ |
| Are they well heated and ventilated? | \_\_\_\_ | \_\_\_\_ |
| Are they light, clean, and attractive? | \_\_\_\_ | \_\_\_\_ |
| Are there chalkboards and bulletin boards? | \_\_\_\_ | \_\_\_\_ |
| Is there enough furniture? | \_\_\_\_ | \_\_\_\_ |
| Is the furniture the correct size? | \_\_\_\_ | \_\_\_\_ |
| Is there good lighting throughout? | \_\_\_\_ | \_\_\_\_ |
| Is there enough space to hang coats and hats? | \_\_\_\_ | \_\_\_\_ |
| Are there adequate restrooms? | \_\_\_\_ | \_\_\_\_ |
| Are there sufficient exits? | \_\_\_\_ | \_\_\_\_ |
| Is there adequate storage room? | \_\_\_\_ | \_\_\_\_ |
| Is there a library? | \_\_\_\_ | \_\_\_\_ |
| Is there adequate filing space? | \_\_\_\_ | \_\_\_\_ |
| Is parking space adequate? | \_\_\_\_ | \_\_\_\_ |
| Are plans being made for improvement? | \_\_\_\_ | \_\_\_\_ |

# KEEPING ON TARGET

## *11*

The Sunday School ministry target is to fulfill Christ's Great Commission of making disciples. Recent studies in the field of Christian education have suggested several worthy standards that need to be addressed if the Sunday School is to keep on target and remain in the forefront of church educational ministry. These standards are:

— Recruit staff properly;
— Follow up students;
— Train every teacher;
— Stress Bible memorization;
— Establish and use the church library;
— Accept change as inevitable.

Although each of these standards could be developed into a whole chapter, our goal here is to introduce each one for consideration in your local context.

### *Recruit staff properly*

Recruitment itself is frowned upon by some as unspiritual. Further, contemporary churches have often launched too many programs and created enormous volunteer needs that give way to the desperate conclusion that "any warm body will do." This approach almost always results in teacher burnout and frustration.

The most effective leaders recruit their staff by beginning with a church that encourages service, continues with a coordinated system for contacting prospects, and bathes the whole process in prayer.

## A church that encourages service

This step is perhaps the most difficult to put into place. As we previously discussed, changing the whole church's attitude regarding volunteerism may be required. Change begins with pastors who wholeheartedly support the Sunday School program in pulpit announcements and promotional publications, emphasize service in their sermons, conduct installation and commissioning ceremonies, and use other creative means to further promote service throughout the church program. These include service recognition, staff banquets, notes, and other expressions of appreciation. A church that encourages service must convince the congregation that the only way to obey Christ is through service.

## A coordinated system for contacting prospects

In order to be effective in recruiting staff, some prerequisites are necessary: talent survey questionnaires, a personnel committee, staff job descriptions, and service contracts.

Churches that encourage service use talent search questionnaires in their ministries. This form lists all the possible areas where tasks are needed to effectively accomplish the church's ministries. It provides a way for respondents to indicate whether they have service experience and whether they would be interested in ministering in that area. Often churches distribute these questionnaires in the new members' classes as part of their interviewing process. After tabulating the responses, the names are channeled to the various ministry leaders, or personnel committee, for follow up in their volunteer searches.

The personnel committee is usually made up of persons who are acquainted with the various tasks to be accomplished in church ministry. Because the Sunday School's personnel roster is so large, it may have its own personnel committee which is responsible only to recommend prospects for serving in that ministry. This committee tries to match people to positions for recommending them to the person who conducts the interviews.

People do not usually volunteer for a position without first knowing what they need to do or what qualifications are required to do it effectively. Staff job descriptions define the position and tell the potential volunteer who they report to, delineate the position's responsibilities, and list the needed qualifications.

When contacting prospects for Sunday School ministry, leaders should have a job description ready for them to consider. Presenting this material during their interview tells them that you have thought about their qualifications and background and that you have matched their gifts and talents with a particular position in which they can be effective.

To further avoid volunteer burnout, service contracts provide leaders and volunteers with a written statement of tenure for their commitment. To strengthen the building of staff and teacher/student relationships, no less than one-year appointments are best. Near the end of the contracted period, leaders and staff members can discuss the experience, recommend changes, decide to take a break, or agree to another year of service.

**Bathe the whole process in prayer**
As with all other areas of church ministry, prayer is crucial for a recruitment program to be effective. This process, however, should not be reserved for just the personnel committee or Sunday School leadership, but the entire church leadership team and every church member. For special emphasis, some churches appoint a prayer team. This group is usually comprised of members who are uniquely gifted and committed to intercessory prayer and who agree to pray faithfully for ministry needs.

## Follow up students
Again, if the Sunday School is to maintain its leadership in church educational ministry, it must stress student follow-up. Over the past few decades the teacher/student relationship model was abandoned, then somewhat rediscovered. When asked the definition of a teacher, to many reply "a person who teaches a lesson." Others, however, insist that it is "someone who helps students learn." The latter is the preferred and more biblical concept for it requires more than just lecturing from an instructor's guide. A teacher facilitates students in understanding and applying God's Word.

**Volunteer ministers needed**
Earlier this text stressed the need for teachers to build relationships with students but it bears repeating here for it is so vital to the ongoing effectiveness of Sunday School ministry. Church members, as a whole, have mistakenly adopted the idea that only professional church leaders minister. If the church and its educational ministry are to survive, however, everyone needs to share in the ministry—especially its volunteer leaders and teachers.

Throughout the New Testament the principle of everyone sharing in ministry is stressed. Jesus taught and commissioned the twelve disciples to carry out the task of discipling. This multiplication process thus begun has continued throughout church history and should continue to be adopted in program of today's church.

**Follow-up procedures**
Sunday School leaders need to develop and implement procedures for following up visitors and absentees. Carrying out such a program may require the help of everyone involved in Sunday

School ministry—leaders, teachers, other staff members, and perhaps even the students and their families. It also requires good record keeping and holding everyone accountable to carry out their part in the process.

For this emphasis to be effective, training in student follow-up principles and procedures is necessary. Many staff members do not understand the need for student follow-up, while others are not comfortable visiting in students' homes—especially if their parents are unchurched. Leaders should use staff meetings to discuss student follow-up methodology and provide opportunities to model techniques.

Many teachers lack the time and resources to obtain materials to carry out student follow-up. For this reason Sunday Schools often supply teachers with cards, note paper, and stamps to communicate with visitors and absentees.

## *Train every teacher*

Ways to conduct training have previously been stressed throughout this text. Now the necessary emphasis must be to underscore the content of teacher training. The survival of the Sunday School depends on excellence in these basic elements:

- The teacher's spiritual life
- Developing teachers' confidence and competence
- Becoming a better student of the Bible
- Understanding and getting to know learners
- Student involvement techniques
- Effective teaching methods
- Helping students live their lessons
- Classroom discipline and control
- Extending teaching sessions beyond the classroom
- New communication methods and resources
- Evaluating teaching effectiveness

Obstacles to getting equipping and training started have to be overcome, convenient times need to be determined, and opportunities for implementing it must be planned, promoted, and carried out.

## *Stress Bible memorization*

On the whole, Sunday School students of all ages are memorizing less Scripture than did their counterparts in the past.

### Obstacles to memorizing

What has caused this serious erosion in the ability to memorize God's Word? First, in the last few decades Christian education publishing companies have emphasized the production of beautifully-designed activity supplements but very little that promotes memorizing God's Word. Much of the up-to-date memorization aids incorporate musical techniques, which speak to only a portion of the learning styles in a typical classroom.

Second, the proliferation of modern language translations has also complicated the memorization process. Previous generations had only one or perhaps two translation options available. Today there are several possibilities and not all generations share the same preference.

Third, everyone is busy. Today it seems as if the urgent always crowds out the important. Keeping up with ambitious family and individual schedules often does not provide for spending time in God's Word. Both mothers and fathers work full-time and their children's schedules are filled with school, community, artistic, and athletic activities.

Fourth, many feel that only children can memorize, yet adults can learn telephone numbers, sports players' averages, and many other trivial facts. What prevents them from learning God's Word? Others feel that since Bibles and Bible reference materials are readily available, memorizing Scripture is not necessary. If Bible content is needed, it can be easily accessed. These attitudes come with hidden dangers. Although manuals are available for almost every pupose, product and service today, memorizing basic information often helps get us through emergency situations. Having God's Word hidden in our hearts can feed our souls, deliver us from temptation, and help us witness to others in any situation.

**Corrective procedures**

For Sunday Schools to thrive, they need to adopt the premise that Bible memorization is important and possible even with today's obstacles. How can church educational leaders reverse negative trends?

Again, it may begin with the attitude of the leadership. Pastors, superintendents, and all educational staff members need to demonstrate the value of Bible memorization. Some churches and Sunday Schools have done this by selecting a theme verse each year and a key verse each month. Others use published memory programs and reward those who show achievement. Along with adopting yearly themes and monthly verses, be sure to also provide creative ideas to use available time for memorizing.

If the use of various translations is an obstacle, try to adopt one translation for all corporate use. Although churches and Sunday Schools cannot and should not legislate the use of only one translation for personal study, they can be sure only one translation is available in church pews and classrooms. When general funds are not available for purchasing new Bibles, some churches have made it a special project. Most Sunday Schools award Bibles to new members or to all students achieving a particular grade level. If this is the case, always provide them with the adopted version.

Being accountable to one another also promotes memorization. Because all Christians are part of the family of God, they sometimes need other family members' encouragement and direction to accomplish the Father's will. One individual or program may not be able to accomplish Bible memorization alone, but working together in households, pairs, and study groups could make the needed difference.

## Establish and use the church library

Adequate libraries build solid, growing, and prosperous educational programs. Some church libraries are used regularly while others go unused or never even established. What makes the difference?

Again, having leaders who care about and promote its use is one important factor. Locate an effective library and behind it you usually find effective leaders promoting and administering it. If you find someone who really cares about books and their use in ministry, many times almost nothing else is needed. A degree in library science is not as important a qualification for the church librarian as much as ownership of the library program and dedication to Christian literature.

Other factors contributing to the library's effectiveness are: visible location, convenient hours, diversified collection, regular promotion, and adequate funding.

For those Sunday Schools that have never had a library, begin one now. It may have to start small, perhaps in a joint location with the media center, but once it is established, adequately staffed, and regularly promoted, it will soon begin to grow. Even if funding is not available, many Sunday School libraries have begun by asking people to contribute books from their private collections and have built from there. Often special offerings and bequests can also be used for library development.

Libraries are essential to Sunday School growth and effectiveness. As with other essential elements of the program, it needs to be part of the regular church educational budget.

## Accept change as inevitable

As the old saying goes, "Nothing is more constant than the need to change." This is true if Sunday Schools are to continue to grow in the future. Things cannot continue to be done in the same way simply because, "we've always done it that way." As in almost every other aspect of life, changes are inevitable in Sunday School ministry. Today most people drive cars rather than walk, many prefer e-mail or FAX machines rather than waiting for the mail, and everyone uses indoor plumbing rather than the outside variety. Changes, when they are handled properly, are usually helpful rather than destructive.

Changes present problems when they come faster and more frequently than people have been prepared for. As pointed out earlier in this text, the Lord's Great Commission to the church and its educational ministry given nearly 2,000 years ago has not changed. While this goal is timeless, changes in culture and society require Sunday Schools to continually make revisions in the ways they accomplish it.

"Is this change really necessary?" Sunday School leaders need to be sure they can answer this question when they present a new idea. If the staff and students are confident in the leadership and understand the reasons behind the change, they will probably not resist changes in the ways the Sunday School seeks to carry out its biblical mandate to make disciples.

## Summary

In order for Sunday School ministry to stay on target in the future, several principles and goals need to be adopted. These include: recruiting staff properly, regularly following up students, training every teacher, stressing Bible memorization, establishing and using the church library, and accepting change.

Many of these goals will only be achieved if the whole church and educational staff work together and create an atmosphere throughout the church that stresses the importance of the Sunday School and in serving Christ in ministry.

## For Further Discussion

1. What standards will help the Sunday School to keep on target in the future?
2. Why does the "any warm body will do" principle usually create teacher burnout and frustration?
3. Why are teachers and other educational staff reluctant to follow up some visitors and absentees?
4. Outline the steps for establishing a new church library and/or resource center.
5. What usually causes changes to be resisted in church educational ministry?

## For Application

1. Choose one of the standards for Sunday School ministry mentioned in this chapter and develop a plan for implementing it in your program.
2. Of the six standards outlined in this chapter, evaluate with other leaders and staff members in your Sunday School which one is most needed in your program and discuss what is necessary to introduce it.

# PATTERNS FOR THE FUTURE

## *12*

The preceding chapters have described the Sunday School's history and current status. It has had an exciting and effective ministry of bringing children, youth, and adults into a saving knowledge of Jesus Christ, enriching their Christian lives, and preparing them to serve Christ. God has used the Sunday School in the past and continues to use it today.

If the Sunday School expects to remain the front runner for local church Christian education, it cannot rest on past accomplishments. It must continue pressing forward to keep up with the changing educational scene. Sunday Schools should evaluate their current programs to determine those elements that are advancing them toward their goals and those that could be modified in favor of more up-to-date techniques and activities.

Both outside influences and developing issues must be considered as the Sunday School plans for the future. Current strengths need to be preserved and future trends understood. A number of current conditions will have a direct impact upon the appearance and character of the Sunday School as the new century progresses.

### *Outside influences*

Changes outside the Sunday School strongly affect its ministry. Sunday Schools that incorporate change to meet present needs have always had the strongest impact. Sunday Schools of the future must respond to the following developments if they are to continue to fulfill Christ's Great Commission.

## Erosion of traditional values

At the end of the 1980s, trend spotters were predicting that the 90s would be a decade of returning to traditional values. In looking back on these reports, however, indicators revealed this did not happen as widespread as predicted. Polls revealed fewer people in society felt organized religion was an important part of their lives. Consequently, society's values reflected more people favoring ethical conduct contrary to tradtional Christian values. Bringing such attitudes into the new millennium is evidence enough the Sunday School is still needed and must continually strive to find better ways of communicating the biblical philosophy of life.

## Decline in literacy

Educational institutions continually report a rapid decline in reading levels among their constituencies. As a result, publishers are constantly lowering their reading levels, as well as adjusting their formats to accommodate the functionally illiterate. The anguishing national debt and continual cuts in governmental spending programs designed to combat this problem are often found to be too costly or ineffective in stopping the erosion.

The problem of illiteracy is a present one and it will continue to plague the Sunday School. Curriculum materials have not been able to keep up with growing issues. New theories on learning styles are slowly incorporated in church curriculum. Many students have difficulty reading and understanding their lessons. The same problems also affect their ability to read and understand the Bible.

## Increase in educational options

In the past two decades, many families have found the education offered through their public schools to be inadequate. Several approaches to augment learning have impacted society and the church alike.

Regional economic depression, socio-political pressures, profound exercise of religious freedom, and many other reasons have contributed to Christian families banding together to establish Christian day schools. Other families, who cannot afford alternative education, and have at least one parent at home, have opted to home school their own children. Both of these educational formats allow greater freedom to select quality curriculum and teach from a biblical perspective. The Bible becomes a prominent study source.

Since most of the children who attend Christian schools or are home schooled also enroll in church educational programs, new challenges are created for the Sunday School. Christian day school and home-schooled students are generally more proficient in Bible knowledge than students attending public schools; hence imbalances are created. The Sunday School will need to be sensitive to this issue and flexible in planning lesson activities.

### Shifting adult population

Sunday Schools must develop a new emphasis on adult education. Statistical surveys indicate a steady demographic shift. Ethnic groups are prominent in nearly all communities. Middle-aged adults have brought blended-family lifestyles to the church. The older adult population has clearly defined expectations also.

As a result, most churches are experiencing increased adult enrollment. Many Sunday Schools have reorganized to accommodate larger and more diverse adult groups and have begun to redirect their programs to minister more effectively. These shifts have required a change in classroom techniques, lesson content, and organizational methodology.

With larger adult groups, the range of interests also multiplies. All these interests cannot be served in one large adult class. Sunday Schools will need to provide for smaller group studies. These studies will be on an elective basis and might include Bible book studies, a current Christian book, or topical area in Christian living. Groupings might also be arranged to focus on the needs and interests of adults in a particular age group.

### Interest in spiritual growth

Although traditional values in society are continuing to decline, Christians, in general, are showing a renewed interest in spiritual things. More and more self-help books are being published and many study courses have been developed. Even secular publications include articles about people who claim to have had spiritual experiences.

This desire for spiritual growth needs to be cultivated. The yearning for spiritual awareness indicates a need to go beyond a basic knowledge of biblical facts to deeply meaningful life application. Christians will expect to be challenged by their Sunday School classes, not just entertained or informed.

### Use of technology

As more and more students become computer-literate and job-related tasks are performed on computers, people will expect most teaching and learning to be technologically implemented. Since the Sunday School's discipling goal requires teaching and learning God's Word, people will increasingly require the convenience of computerized products or other time-saving features.

Already various Bible translations are available on computer disks and audio cassettes. Bible learning materials are also emerging which are computer generated and copier reproducible. If they have not already, Sunday Schools need to keep abreast of the marketplace and begin to acquire innovative resources as well as implement computer operations in their educational programs.

Audiovisuals are now firmly established as enhancing communication. Video, once thought a luxury, is now commonplace. Many applications for overhead transparencies still exist. Audio sources now cover every resource category: children's Bible readings, music, self-help, and multimedia presentation.

### Restructuring Christian higher education

Certainly the field of Christian education, and more specifically local church education, is much broader than the Sunday School. What students are studying in institutions of Christian higher education, however, directly impacts what happens in local churches. As with the church, these institutions are engaged in a restructuring era. A greater emphasis is placed on how to administer a variety of educational programs, especially the Sunday School.

Seminaries, which have waned through the years on the philosophical credibility of some Christian education programs, are facing the pragmatic issues presented by pastors and church leaders. As the fields of opportunity broaden, more expertise is being required of local church staffs.

As higher education prepares more students to professionally address these areas, churches must increase the opportunities for service. Leaders who graduate from Christian institutions of higher learning should be strategically placed in all areas of church education, especially the Sunday School. Wherever these graduates can help further a church's ministry, they should be employed and challenged. Even though the Sunday School is a lay ministry working in tandem with church leaders, professional input can better define and implement its educational and philosophical goals.

## Developing issues

The future opportunities for Sunday School ministry are bright with many new emphases on the horizon. Sunday Schools planning for the future need to be aware of changes in these areas.

### The family

Society in general, and Christians in particular, are becoming increasingly alarmed about the breakdown of the family. The sharp increases in divorce, blended families, childhood and teenage delinquency, and both parents working outside the home, have brought about a demand for more attention on the family. Sunday School is an ideal place for this to happen.

It appears clear that traditional family structures are changing quickly and lifestyles will not improve easily. What a challenge for the Sunday School to find ways of better meeting these needs! Teachers should be in close touch with their students' homelife to better direct instruction toward the problems students face.

Another technique being rediscovered is intergenerational learning. This combines various family members in the same class so that students can benefit from the perspectives and experience of all age levels. This option is most successful with topical issues. If all family members participated in the same class, presented their views on the lesson content, and applied the biblical truths to their lives, better communication and sharing might result. If this approach is adopted, a greater variety of materials incorporating the concept of family learning need to be produced. Class size, duration of sessions, and staffing require special attention.

**Mobility and Sunday School attendance**

Families who do not have long-standing roots in the community are more the norm than the exception. Adults are faced with changing careers several times during their working years, often uprooting the family to transfer into new regions.

All families have difficulty scheduling the many events of modern life. It is a new challenge for the Sunday School to keep regular attendance as a priority for its students. With the opportunity to offer more variety in Sunday School programming, leaders will need to adopt goals that can be reached within shorter terms, particularly when rewards are involved. Inevitably, volunteers will demand an adjustment to their obligations toward short-term commitments.

**Bible teaching**

Whenever the central focus of the Sunday School is diverted from the Bible, problems arise. Today, Sunday Schools that stress the truths of God's Word are growing both in numbers and spirituality. When the Bible is faithfully taught and systematically applied to the students' lives, the Sunday School grows and becomes more effective. Campaigns and contests may increase attendance for a time, but long-lasting results stem from offering biblical answers to present-day challenges.

As in the past and present, the Bible must be kept as the central theme and focus of the Sunday School's message. Even though methods for teaching change to accommodate people's interests, the Bible must remain the only source of faith and practice.

**Creative resources**

The quality of curriculum materials for use in the Sunday School continues to improve with technology. Denominational and independent publishing companies, using the most up-to-date materials and methods, are producing attractive, creative, and economical materials for every level of the Sunday School. Along with the traditional guides and quarterlies, many elective studies and easy-to-use multimedia resources are increasingly available for use in Sunday School. New curriculums are being developed for further instruction to special education and multi-ethnic students. Curriculum producers have proven that they have the expertise to develop and design effective educational materials for implementing the new programs of the future.

### Leadership training

Increasingly, church and Sunday School administrators have seen the benefits of training their teachers and leaders. As a result, a variety of leadership training materials are available. More and more Sunday Schools are emphasizing and conducting teacher equipping and training programs.

The future challenges for leadership training are as far-reaching as the number of possibilities for Sunday School. As Sunday School ministries change, so also will leadership training. Where structure and roles of Sunday School classes change, more leaders and teachers with different skills and techniques will be needed.

## Summary

What will Sunday Schools be like in the future? No one can really answer that question. Only limiting honest evaluation will stifle Sunday School's growth. An innovative use of resources will not only rejuvenate any antiquated images of Sunday School, but will restructure its teaching methods without compromising doctrine. With careful analysis of past experiences and insightful planning for the future, the Sunday School can continue to grow stronger and be more effective. As an instrument for leading people to Christ, the Sunday School remains a foundational base to nurture people in the faith and prepare them for future service.

## For Further Discussion

1. Why do you think the Sunday School faced problems when its central focus strayed away from the Bible?
2. Why has Sunday School attendance dropped in many mainline denominational churches?
3. What effect has the decline in quality of public school education had on the Sunday School?
4. How has the Sunday School adapted multimedia and computerized approaches to learning?
5. What accounts for the recent changes in the structure of Sunday School attendance?
6. How can the Sunday School better minister to families?
7. What can the Sunday School do to capitalize on the increased number of Christian education graduates?
8. Why is the shifting adult population an asset rather than a liability for the Sunday School?

## *For Application*

1.  Evaluate the flexibility of your own Sunday School. How many significant changes have you made in recent years? What areas might still benefit from change?

2.  Write a letter this week to some organization responsible for helping your Sunday School succeed. It might be a denominational Christian education office or a publisher. Ask key questions regarding some problems you are presently facing.

3.  Spend some time over the next few weeks designing a basic Bible test which can be administered to students who have spent several years in your Sunday School. Balance the questions between Old and New Testaments and gear the test to about the ninth or tenth grade level. Ask students throughout the Sunday School (or perhaps a random sample) to complete the test and indicate only their ages, not their names. Evaluate the results and grade your Sunday School on the effectiveness of communicating Bible content.

# BIBLIOGRAPHY

Barna, George. *The Frog in the Kettle*. Ventura, CA: Regal Books, 1990.

_____. *User Friendly Churches*. Ventura, CA: Regal Books, 1991.

Benson, Clarence H. *The Sunday School in Action*. Chicago, IL: Moody Press, 1932, 1941.

Brown, Lowell E. and Reed, Bobbie. *Your Sunday School Can Grow*. Glendale, CA: Regal Books, 1974.

Carlson, Gregory C. *Understanding Teaching, Effective Biblical Teaching for the 21st Century*. Wheaton, IL: Evangelical Training Association, 1998.

Clark, Robert E.; Johnson, Lin; Sloat, Allyn K., eds. *Christian Education: Foundations for the Future*. Chicago: Moody Press, 1991.

Cionca, John R. *Solving Church Education's Ten Toughest Problems*. Wheaton: Victor Books, 1990.

Gangel, Kenneth. *Christian Educators Handbook on Teaching*. Wheaton: Victor Books, 1988.

_____. *You can be an Effective Sunday School Superintendent*. Wheaton: Victor Books, 1981.

Hemphill, Ken. *Revitalizing the Sunday Morning Dinosaur*. Nashville: Broadman and Holman Publishers, 1996.

Hendricks, Howard. *Teaching to Change Lives*. Portland: Multnomah Press, 1987.

Kilbreth, Leon. *Building on Basics of Chruch Growth*. Herrin, IL: Leon Kilbreth Evangelistic Association.

LeFever, Marlene. *Learning St...* You to Teach. Colorad... Company, 1995.

Pierson, Jim and Kort... *from Ministry with...* nati: Standard Publish...

Plueddemann, James E. Lois E. ... *tian*. Wheaton: Victor Books, 1...

Schaller, Lyle E. *Effective Church Plannu...* Press, 1979.

_____. *The Multiple Staff and the Larger Chu...* Abingdon Press, 1980.

Smith, Sid. 10 Super Sunday Schools in the Black Comm... Nashville: Broadman Press, 1986.

Thigpen, Jonathan, ed. *Teaching Techniques, Revitalizing Methodology*. Wheaton, IL: Evangelical Training Association, 2000.

Towns, Elmer. *Sunday School Encyclopedia*. Wheaton, IL: Tyndale House Publishers, 1993.

_____. *The Super Superintendent*. Denver: Accent Publishing, 1980.

Zuck, Roy B. *Spirit-filled Teaching*. Nashville: Word Publishing, 1998.

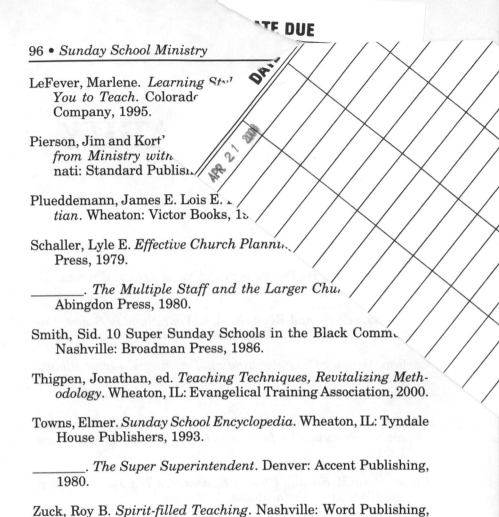